The School: An Organizational Analysis

BLACKIE BOOKS ON ORGANIZATIONAL ANALYSIS

The Concept of Organization
The Hospital: An Organizational Analysis
The School: An Organizational Analysis
The University: An Organizational Analysis

The School:
An Organizational Analysis

Stephen J. Bennett

BLACKIE: Glasgow and London

0 216 89743 2 (Paperback)
0 216 89704 1 (Hardback)

Blackie and Son Limited
Bishopbriggs, Glasgow G64 2NZ
5 Fitzhardinge Street, London WH1 0DL

Printed by Thomson Litho, East Kilbride, Scotland

Contents

Introduction

This book is presented as an introduction to the analysis of schools as organizations. It is concerned with the consequences which follow from the fact of organization rather than from the fact of teaching. Schools depend not simply on teaching skills, but also on a whole range of non-teaching activity, such as decisions about objectives, the provision of resources, the setting up of structural arrangements, and the control and evaluation of organizational activities. As a result, much of the behaviour of teachers in schools is not involved directly with teaching. The relevance of organizational analysis is that it can attempt to illuminate and explain this behaviour.

The importance of organizations has been increasingly recognized in recent years. In the United States in particular, there is a history of organizational research which goes back to the beginning of the century. However, both in this country and in the United States, the main impetus for such research has come from industrial and commercial interests and the main focus of the research has often been on managerial problems.

It is clear, however, that if we are to engage in a study of organizations, we must include organizations other than industrial and commercial ones. Furthermore, there is no reason to restrict the study to those aspects of organizations defined as managerially relevant. Indeed, there are good reasons for not doing so. Organizations are powerful and affect the lives not only of all who work in them, but also of other people who may not be directly connected with them at all. Investment decisions taken by large international corporations are perhaps the most obvious example. Schools, however, are also powerful. Individual schools affect the lives of thousands of children, influencing the kind of education they receive and the type of career they will follow.

Efforts should certainly be made to solve the management problems of schools so that they may function more efficiently and so that children may receive better educations, although we should be aware of the wide variety of interpretations which can be put on phrases such as 'function more efficiently' and 'better educations'. Efforts should also be made to assess the organizational consequences for children of their stay in schools. After all, much more happens in schools than the teaching of mathematics, English, history and science. The very administrative decisions taken in schools affect not only what is to be taught, when, how, where, under what conditions, and by whom, but also matters such as standards of dress, and length of hair which may, at first sight, have no obvious relation to teaching and learning mathematics or English. Aspects of behaviour, such as smoking, and ways of addressing adults are also controlled. Some of these decisions may be justified by claims that teachers are *in loco parentis* although the school may insist on adherence to rules even when parents make it clear that they do not agree with the rules. Other decisions may be justified by reference to the good name of the school. Occasionally, no attempt will be made at justification. It may be stated, for example, that certain clothes are 'not suitable' for school. In other words, as a result of being caught up in this particular organization children are taught behaviour that is acceptable in the organization.

Most people, of course, have little idea and even less say as to what goes on in schools. All children are supposed to receive some sort of tuition and for most people this means sending their children to the local school. Schools have a duty to see that their pupils attend regularly and if they do not the local education authority may be informed, and eventually legal proceedings will be taken in an effort to ensure the child's attendance at school. Parents, then, have to send their children to school but they have little influence over what happens to them when they get there. Even the choice of school is usually decided for them by arrangements made by the local education authority. The kinds of classes the children join, the subjects they are taught, the rules they have to obey, and the punishments they may suffer if they are judged to have disobeyed the rules, all such matters will be decided largely without reference to the parents of the children involved.

Legitimate questions may be asked about these arrangements. Is it right, for example, that so many matters which vitally affect a child's life should be decided upon without reference to the child's parents? Teachers, of course, have been trained to teach and we have to be content to leave the education of our children, in areas about which we know little or nothing, to others who are more expert. However, administrative arrangements in schools and the rules to which children have to adhere are based on ideas of what is right and wrong, proper and improper, and these are ideas about which no one can lay claim to absolute knowledge or professional authority. What is more they are ideas about which all parents should be concerned, or at least have a right to be concerned. Education committees, of course, are made up partly of elected councillors who are theoretically responsible to the electorate. Presumably if we don't like what is going on in our schools we can change our representatives. However, we must still ask whether these arrangements are adequate. Do parents find that councillors are responsive to their wishes? Have councillors sufficient time to devote to individual queries concerning particular schools? Are councillors elected on the basis of what happens in schools? To what extent should schools be responsive to parents' wishes? What role should parents play in schools? What are the decisions about which parents should be consulted?

At the present time, many of the assumptions on which existing arrangements are based are being challenged. Some people are asking whether we need schools at all. It may be that the undesirable consequences of schools as we understand them, are so great that they outweigh the desirable ones. Can children be said genuinely to receive an education in schools? The answer to this question will hinge on what we mean by 'education'. Certainly there is no agreement about what kind of education children should receive. Are the traditional subjects taught in schools still useful? What other subjects should be taught? What are the criteria by which we decide what should be taught in schools? How are we to decide whether schools should be involved in sex education, for example? Should schools attempt to teach moral or social education, and what would be the advantages and disadvantages of this? There has been some controversy recently as to whether politics should be taught in schools. Although the establishment and funding of schools are political issues, people are suspicious of political influences in schools. An example of this occurred recently in the case of the schools conferences organized by the Conservative Party. On the other hand when children leave school, or shortly afterwards, they are likely to be faced with political choices at general and local elections. It could be argued that they should receive some sort of preparation for deciding about those choices. Undoubtedly there would be a great deal of disagreement as to the kind of preparation. Who would be involved and what political ideas would be discussed? The three main political parties would be assured of their place in the sun, but what about the Communist Party, the Scottish Nationalist Party and Plaid Cymru, to say nothing of the National Front?

Questions are also being asked about the extent to which schools should prepare children to live in the areas from which they come. Education has traditionally been seen as a passport for the working-class child out of his native area.

But what about those children who fail to obtain a passport? What have the schools to offer them? This raises the question of the school's relationship with its local situation. To what extent should schools remain separate from the local community and to what extent should they involve themselves in the community? What kind of involvement would be acceptable?

All in all, it is an exciting time for schools. There are new developments in teaching methods and new ideas about the content of traditional subjects. There are also moves away from the usual subject pattern, and towards the teaching of issues to which a number of subjects can contribute. Teacher training is another area about which there is a great deal of discussion. The James report on teacher education and training is an example of this. Management training for teachers is also becoming increasingly important. New courses and departments in colleges and universities concerned with educational management and administration are appearing all over the country. There is even a British Educational Administration Society which has among its aims 'To advance the practice of educational administration and to this end to promote high standards in the teaching of, and research into, educational administration in the United Kingdom'.[1]

Many of the developments which are taking place have been concerned with organizational issues. These range from the setting up of new kinds of schools to developments in the internal structure of schools. Some new kinds of schools have derived from a dissatisfaction with existing schools on the part of parents and teachers. Attempts have been made by parents to run their own schools. Teachers have set up 'free schools' which are not formally connected with the official education system and which are based on a different philosophy of education. Other kinds of schools are a result of official experimentation. Six-year schools, four-year schools, two- and three-year schools, middle schools, senior schools and sixth-form colleges, are all examples of this. These developments have been imposed on an existing pattern of great diversity of schools. There are, for example, among schools maintained by local authorities, nursery, primary and secondary schools. Secondary schools may be comprehensive, grammar or secondary modern schools. In addition there are private schools, direct-grant schools and special schools. Schools may be mixed or single-sex, religiously based, day schools or boarding schools. It would clearly be cumbersome to attempt to discuss all types of schools, and so reference will be made, in the main, to the six-year, mixed, local authority maintained comprehensive school.

Each of these different types of school has its own peculiar organizational problems and its own particular internal structural arrangements. Again there is great diversity of structure even within the same types of schools. Certain general issues have been raised about school structure. There have been calls for more staff participation in the running of schools. How is this to work? In large schools with a hundred or more teachers, how are decisions to be taken if everyone is to be involved? What kinds of decisions should staff be involved in? Which decisions would they want to be involved in? What are the advantages of greater staff participation? How is it to be reconciled to the notion of the headmaster having responsibility for what happens in his school? Are more mature notions needed as school organizations have become much bigger than ever they were? Now that we have made the discovery of the importance of organizational consequences, are other arrangements needed to cope with these consequences? The collective wisdom of all teachers in a school may be more difficult to get at but it may be more useful. Would we run a greater danger by relying on the collective wisdom than by relying on the judgement and abilities of one man?

The internal organization of pupils also varies a great deal. Many schools still allocate pupils to classes on the basis of some assessment of their ability. Others are experimenting with mixed-ability classes, sometimes only for administrative purposes, but sometimes also for teaching purposes. There are also experiments with different types of pastoral organization, such as house groups and year groups. Again, there have been calls for more pupil participation in the running of schools. Some schools have established structures of pupil committees, such as year committees and school councils. Pupils are also sometimes included in joint staff-pupil committees which deal with some aspects of school life. There are important issues here. To what extent should pupils be involved in decision-making in the school? What sort of decisions could they appropriately be consulted about? What kinds of decisions should be left to them? To what extent should pupil behaviour be controlled? Are only senior pupils to be consulted? To what extent are the calls for greater pupil participation a reaction to bureaucratic rigidity and old-fashioned notions about childhood on the part of headmasters and staff? There is clearly a contrast between the freedom allowed to young people who leave school at the minimum leaving age and the strictly controlled activities of young people who stay on at school. Similarly, there is a contrast between the strict control exercised (in some schools at least) over the behaviour of sixth-formers and the adult status accorded to them a few months later when they leave school. To what extent is the strictness of the control an adequate preparation for life outside the school?

Finally, it is necessary to note one additional development which is undoubtedly an organizational development, and that is the trend to large schools. This trend has been justified in terms of the kinds of resources which a large school can provide, such as lavish material resources and also a wide variety of courses. Another reason has been the belief that comprehensive schools have to be large in order to provide a reasonably sized sixth-form, although this is increasingly open to doubt. At the present time we do not know enough about the problems which might be associated with large schools. Nor do we know what can be done to mitigate the problems, although efforts are being made in terms of dividing the school into smaller units with which pupils may find it easier to identify. There are, of course, also consequences for the staff relationships and formal staff structures.

When this book was written I was engaged in research into the school as an organization. Although this is in no sense a report on that research, I would like to record my gratitude to the staff of the schools which participated for their co-operation and kindness.

I would also like to thank Roy Wilkie, who has been a good teacher and a good friend, for asking me to write this book and providing extensive theoretical criticism and stylistic improvements. Tom Keenoy, Bill Sang and David Bradley read parts of an earlier draft, as did Keith Newton with whom I discussed many of the ideas for the book, and Nick Perry, who has given me friendly advice and encouragement during the course of my research. My wife, Mary, provided comprehensive support throughout the writing of this book, even to the extent of reading and commenting on several drafts. Love, as they say, hath no bounds. Finally, thanks to Mrs Patricia McTaggart, who typed most of an earlier draft, and to Mrs Mary Allan, who typed the final version.

[1] 'Educational Administration Bulletin', published by the British Educational Administration Society, Vol. 1, No. 2, Spring 1973, p. 53.

CHAPTER 1

The Environment

It may seem strange to begin a discussion of the school as an organization with an examination of the environment of the school. The environment, after all, consists by definition of those objects and circumstances which are outside the school. In practice, however, it is very difficult in the case of the school (as with other organizations) to decide where the school stops and the environment starts. Another reason for beginning in this way is that the environment sets the scene. Many of the activities of a school can be explained by reference to outside influences.

The environment of a school is complex, as are the school's relations with that environment. In the first place, there is the wider social background in which the school is situated, the society to which the school belongs. Secondly, there are the wider administrative or educational systems of which most schools are a part. Thirdly, there is the immediate locale in which the school finds itself. Lastly, we have to note that the school is affected by these different aspects of the environment in different ways and engages with the environment on different levels.

The first aspect, then, is the wider social background of the school which wields its influence in a number of ways. Each society has its own moral standards, customs and beliefs, and these will affect the schools which develop, the education which the schools attempt to provide, the people who teach in the schools, and the children who become pupils in the schools. That this is so is clear from the differing education systems which are to be found in other countries and also in the historical changes which have occurred in education in our own country. The standards, customs and beliefs of a society will influence the way in which teachers regard children, the expectations they have of them, and the things which children are expected to learn. In this sense, the curriculum is clearly located in the culture of a society, as are the methods used in teaching and the ways in which judgement is made as to whether children have reached a required standard of learning.

Children's reactions to their teachers and to what they are expected to learn will also be culturally determined. Social factors affect children's responses to school in different ways. A child's readiness to learn in school will be influenced by circumstances such as whether his family is working-class or middle-class, the occupations of his parents, how affluent the family is, and the particular history and experiences of the family. The son of a headmaster or a university teacher will have advantages in coping with school work, which may be denied to the son of a working-class family whose parents have had only a minimum of formal education. This is not to say that the middle-class child will always do better, only that he starts with advantages. The political and economic situation of the country will also affect children's readiness to learn. In new and developing countries where education is directly related to economic well-being, exclusion from school could be seen as a punishment, in marked contrast to the attitude of most children in this country. The factors which affect children's responses to their teachers will also affect the teachers' responses to them. In this connection, the change to comprehensive education is relevant, as many of the teachers who, at present, teach in comprehensive schools have been trained and have received their early experience in a different system. Former grammar school teachers may, in some cases, be apprehensive and even hostile to children who would, under the old system, have gone to a secondary modern school. They may react unfavourably to the 'rough kids' who come from an area from which most children previously went to such a school.

The class structure and the occupational structure of the society will also affect schools. A society with a highly pronounced and strictly maintained class structure may have different schools for the members of the different classes. Even in our own society, where the class structure can be said to have changed greatly, relics of an older system persist. The occupational structure is important because to some extent the schools train people for future occupations. This is obvious in the vocational training aspects of school education, although schools form only a part of a wider system which is concerned with training and which includes further education colleges, universities, colleges of education and polytechnics. Over a long period, industrial and scientific changes created a need for a working population with a certain level of skill and general education and this, together with changing ideas about the right of every person to some sort of an education, led to an expansion of the education system and eventually to compulsory education for a statutorily determined length of time. Nowadays it is quite common for governments to demand more scientists, more technologists or more teachers. Schools will take into account such demands and the probable career opportunities they represent in guiding pupils into careers.

Contemporary technology is perhaps the most striking environmental factor at work. The amount and cost of the machinery in the metalwork department of a modern school are examples of this. So are the language laboratories, closed circuit television experiments, and the use of radio and television broadcasts on a national scale.

Apart from influencing the methods and content of teaching, the culture of a society also affects the kinds of people teachers are, their behaviour to each other and also, very importantly, their behaviour in the presence of children. This will have an effect on children's perceptions of what adults are like, of what it means to be an adult. Teachers are not the only adult models children have but they are an important and influential group. Since children learn adult behaviour by observing adults, the way that teachers behave shapes the way their pupils will behave when they in turn become adults. Parents, of course, are also adult models, and the family is perhaps the most important 'environmental' influence as far as children are concerned. It is as well to remember that the family is also an 'agency of education', far more important than the school in its long-term effects. The relationship between the school and the families of its pupils, therefore, will be critical.

The second aspect of the environment is the public education system to which most schools in Wales, Scotland and England belong. They have relations with the government departments responsible for education in the three countries and with the local education authorities, the examining boards, the universities, colleges, teachers' professional organizations, and other bodies involved in the system. The school's relations with government departments, local authorities and examining boards make it difficult to think of the school as an organization in the usual sense of the term. In some ways the school is so closely connected with these aspects of its 'environment' as to make it difficult to decide where the organization ends and the environment begins. By contrast, in the modern business organization, policy, procedures and objectives are decided within the organization, by the shareholders (in so far as they can be considered part of the organization) or by the board of directors, or by individual managers or other employees, or by interactions between them. This is not to say that the organization does not have to take account of environmental influences such as laws, governmental regulations, trade unions, professional organizations, customer reactions and other sources of influence. The organization may, of course, be owned by another organization, in which case certain issues of policy and procedures may be decided by the owning organization. But in such a case it is quite easy and certainly acceptable to see the first organization as part of a larger organization. As far as the school is concerned, on the other hand, there are centres of power located outside the school which have a direct bearing on the procedures and policies adopted by the school. Yet it does not make much sense to think of the school as part of the larger organization consisting of the educational system to which the school belongs. The wider educational system is too diffuse for that and the links between the different parts are too varied in type.

It might be helpful to think of some of these bodies as providing the legitimizing context for schools, for without their consent individual schools cannot exist. Parliamentary legislation provides the authority under which schools are built, staffed and financed. Three Secretaries of State are responsible to Parliament for education in the three countries. In Scotland the Secretary of State exercises his responsibility through the Scottish Education Department, in Wales through the Welsh Department of Education, and in England through the Department of Education and Science. These three are concerned with supervising the provision of education by the local authorities. They approve or disapprove local authority schemes for building new schools and changing the character of existing ones, and they are required to maintain a general oversight of educational standards through Her Majesty's Inspectorate. In other words, their effect is in the main supervisory and regulatory, and their influence falls mainly on the local authority. The exception here is in the case of the Inspectorate who visit individual schools and may make recommendations to individual headmasters and teachers.

The local education authorities have a much more direct influence on individual schools. One commentator includes among their main duties:

1. to provide full-time primary and secondary education in schools sufficient in number, character and equipment to give to all pupils instruction and training appropriate to their ages, abilities and aptitudes. This includes nursery schools, special schools and boarding educations as appropriate;
2. to maintain approved voluntary schools;
3. to maintain all schools according to standards specified by the Secretary of State;
4. to make instruments and articles of management or government for county primary and secondary schools;
5. to produce development plans for their areas;
6. to make arrangements for religious instruction according to the Act;
7. to ascertain what special education treatment is needed;
8. to ensure that all parents cause their children to be suitably educated;
9. to provide medical inspection and treatment.

"Their powers include:
1. establishing new schools, maintaining as county schools schools formerly independent or voluntary, and ceasing to maintain schools;
2. grouping schools under one management;
3. controlling secular instruction in county schools, and voluntary schools (except aided secondary schools);
4. controlling the appointment of teachers (except for special arrangements, notably those for religious education in voluntary schools);
5. controlling, within limits, the use of voluntary school premises;

6. providing board and lodging, clothing and making other special arrangements for educating children with special needs;
7. regulating the part-time employment of schoolchildren;
8. inspecting, through their officers, educational establishments maintained by them;
9. making grants and meeting expenses of pupils and students for whose education they are responsible."[2]

The situation is similar in Scotland as can be seen from the following.

"Education authorities have conferred on them by statute a range of powers and duties, of which the following are important examples: the adequate and efficient provision of all forms of primary, secondary, and further education; the provision of adequate facilities for recreation and social and physical training; the provision of special education for handicapped pupils; the provision of a child guidance service; provision for religious observance and instruction in schools; provision, free of charge, of books, writing materials, stationery, mathematical instruments and other necessary articles; the enforcement of attendance at school; provision, in the case of a county, of books for general reading; provision and maintenance of hostels for pupils attending day schools; the payment of bursaries and other allowances to persons over age 15 attending schools and further education centres; the granting in certain cases of exemption from the obligation to attend school to pupils over 14 years of age; the payment of fees of pupils attending schools at which fees are payable; the provision of transport or payment of travelling expenses; provision of . . . a midday meal; provision of clothing for pupils inadequately clad; provision for the medical inspection and treatment of pupils; the appointment and dismissal of teachers;

the making of by-laws with regard to the employment of children"[3]

Other organizations contribute to the legitimitizing context. The examination boards control the major aspects of the examination system. This means that they have a substantial influence on what is taught in schools, at least in courses leading to public examinations. Examinations, and thereby the content of courses, are standardized and individual schools have no say in this standardization, except in so far as individual teachers are connected with the examining boards in some capacity. In Wales, the Welsh Joint Education Committee, which acts as an examining board, also involves itself in other activities, such as initiating research and commissioning textbooks.

In Scotland, there is the General Teaching Council which is responsible for the certification of teachers. All Scottish teachers in local authority schools must register with the Council. The Council has disciplinary powers and can remove teachers' names from its register, thereby making it impossible for any local authority in Scotland to employ them. The Council may also make proposals to the Secretary of State for Scotland with regard to standards of training for teachers.

In addition, there is the Schools Council which concerns itself with research into curriculum matters, although in a purely advisory capacity. It also advises the Secretary of State on examinations. A comparable body in Scotland is the Consultative Committee on the Curriculum.

These last two bodies are concerned with the creation and diffusion of ideas throughout the educational system. Other bodies are also involved in this. There are research units such as the National Foundation for Educational Research and those at the universities and colleges of education. In-service training organizations and professional organizations are relevant here, as are the Inspectorate, local education authority advisers and

inspectors, publishers and, of course, the schools themselves. There are new ideas about what education is or
means, what is the best education for children of differing
abilities and aptitudes, the differences between education
and training, the relevance of vocational training, the place
of social and religious and moral education, and a whole
range of ideas about teaching materials and teaching aids.
New ideas are passed around in all sorts of ways, through
journals, by the Inspectorate, at headmasters' and teachers'
meetings, and these too form part of the environment of
the school.

We should also note that the education system itself
functions against the background of a local and national
political system. The Secretary of State is a politician
and may have had only a minimal connection with
education prior to his appointment. He may also, interest-
ingly enough, have had only a minimal connection with
the system of public schools. G. S. Osborne, writing prior
to 1966, notes the predominance of ministers responsible
for the education service who had been educated at private
schools. This tendency was also apparent in governments
as a whole. Mr Osborne quotes Harold Macmillan:
"Mr. Attlee had three old Etonians in his Cabinet. I
have six. Things are twice as good under the Conser-
vatives".[4]

Party political ideas and pressures are not so apparent
in the everyday life of schools as they are in proposals
to change aspects of the educational system, or in resistance
to such proposals. The move to comprehensive schools
under the last government, against a background of
resistance from local authorities of a different political
persuasion, and, conversely, the resistance by the present
government to proposals from local authorities which
would radically alter the character of grammar schools,
are evidence of this. Schools, of course, are affected by
these ideas and pressures and the difficulties associated
with them. Comprehensive reorganization has meant in

many instances that schools have to use two or more sites which may be some distance apart, or separated by busy roads, or both. This clearly makes life difficult for teachers and pupils and means that there are extra problems which have to be taken into account in the internal organization of the school. Again, because of the resistance to comprehensive education, comprehensive schools sometimes have to co-exist with a grammar school, which affects their intake and their standing in the local community.

The third aspect of the environment is the immediate locale of the school. Is the school situated in, or near to, a local community? Is the community rural or urban? What are the relations between the school and the community? Do the teachers live in the community? What other nearby schools are there, and what are their natures? Do they compete with the school? For a comprehensive school it may be of critical importance whether there is a grammar school operating in its catchment area. What are the relations between the two schools and how are the pupils allocated to each? The existence of private schools nearby will be important for similar reasons. What are the relations between the school and its local feeder primary schools? What effect do these relations have on the way new entrants settle into the secondary school?

Other important local factors might include the presence of religious sectarianism, which may determine the school a child attends, and the existence of a dominant industry or firm which may have the pick of the school leavers.

What kind of neighbourhood is the school located in? Is it old or new, socially mixed or made up of one predominant class of people? In some places, slums have been pulled down and the inhabitants rehoused in new housing estates in a different area, lacking in social amenities, and also lacking any sense of belonging or community spirit which may have existed previously. A school situated in such an area has problems which a school situated in a more stable and perhaps more socially congenial area will not be faced with. The problem will, in all likelihood, be exacerbated by the fact that the teachers do not live in the area and may feel detached from the problems of the children. In such a situation much will depend on the teachers' reaction to the area and to the difficulties of the children.

Schools with immigrant children have their own peculiar problems. In the first place, there are problems caused by the characteristics or customs of the immigrants themselves. The caste system, for example, may inhibit what would usually be regarded in schools as normal classroom discussions. Some teachers also believe it to be one of the causes of playground conflict. Another example, recently reported in the press, concerned a father who kept his daughter away from school because he feared she would become pregnant. He apparently objected to co-educational schools on the grounds of his faith. Secondly, there are language difficulties. Immigrant pupils may pick up enough English to satisfy the demands of everyday living, but the acquisition of the deeper knowledge of the language necessary for school learning may be much more difficult. Connected with this is the problem of correctly assessing the ability of pupils who have a relatively poor command of the English language. As a consequence of this many immigrant children could be labelled as academically less able. Suggestions have been made for teacher-interpreters to be appointed to schools with a high number of immigrants, and also for immigrants themselves to be encouraged to become teachers. Language problems, of course, are not limited to schools with recent immigrants. The range of idioms to be found within the British Isles may also cause difficulties. Teachers who are new to an area may find difficulty in understanding their pupils' speech, and the pupils may have similar difficulties. A third set of problems is caused by the (perhaps unconscious) attitudes of teachers who may be prejudiced against immigrants, and the bias of teaching materials which refer only to white children and which are concerned with the preoccupations and history of white people. Some schools now run courses in Black Studies as an attempted corrective to this state of affairs. Suggestions have also been made that teachers should receive special training for dealing with immigrant children.

Other conditions bring other problems. Geographical mobility is a characteristic of our society. This creates difficulties for the children who have to change homes and schools. It also creates difficulties for the schools in two ways. In the first place, because they have no personal knowledge of the families they may find it harder to deal with children who are having some sort of trouble. Secondly, teachers are themselves mobile and schools are frequently afflicted by a high teacher turnover rate.

New schools or schools whose characters are radically changed will have to cope with difficulties not faced by more established schools. This may be particularly true of new comprehensive schools. Parents will have a variety of responses to a new comprehensive school based on their own school experiences and the hearsay experiences of others, as well as their opinions about the value of comprehensive education. Parents of 'bright' children may be hostile to the school, fearing a lowering of standards and a sub-standard education for their children.

All schools must have relations with the parents of their pupils. However, the nature of those relations varies widely. Contact with parents may be limited to meeting individual parents to discuss a child's progress or future career in the school. There may be occasional parents' evenings or open days during which parents are encouraged to visit the school and meet the staff and discuss the work of the school and its various departments, and to discuss the progress and prospects of their children. Other schools have parent-teacher associations, or parents' associations. Such groupings have varying degrees of influence on the school. Much depends on the attitude of the school. If it is hostile to parents' organizations, the influence of the parents will be minimal and the meetings of the association may have no relevance to the work of the school. Other schools use such associations to inform parents about what the school is attempting to do and to explain changes in an attempt to gain the support of the parents. In such cases some of the staff of the school may be appointed to a committee of the association and may be instrumental in organizing its activities, obtaining speakers to talk on educational topics, organizing fund-raising events, and so on.

Schools have other kinds of contact with parents. Subject teachers may be approached by parents who are concerned about their children's performance in a certain subject. In a large school, house staff may have more contact with parents than the headmaster, because parents are frequently directed to them as the people who know most about individual children. House staff may establish times outside school hours when they are available to meet parents who are unable to visit the school during school hours.

Parents can also have, or attempt to have, influence in other ways. They may form pressure groups for change, or to resist change, in education. The resistance in Glasgow and Edinburgh to the proposal to put an end to fee-paying schools is a case in point. Parents may object to the schools to which their children are allocated by the local education authority. In some cases they have refused to accept the decision of the local authority and have attempted to run their own schools. These sorts of pressure are perhaps, more usually directed at the wider educational system as in these examples.

So far we have referred in the main to the environment as something which affects the school. The school, however, can also utilize its environment, and to some extent may attempt to neutralize it. Schools invite individuals to give talks to pupils, doctors come to lecture on drugs or sex education, policemen discuss crime and the role of the police, representatives of firms talk about their work and the work of their firms, clergymen take religious assemblies and talk about the place of the church in modern society, and so on. Schools organize educational visits to universities and colleges, factories and shops. Groups of pupils may be involved in visits to hospitals and projects to help old people in their communities. Associations of former pupils may be encouraged to develop contacts with the school for purposes which may include the maintenance of tradition and sentimental contacts, but which may also include the benefits of fund-raising and monetary and other gifts to the school. Meetings may be arranged between the staff of neighbouring schools, particularly where the schools may be linked in some way, as in a primary/ secondary relationship. The purposes of these meetings will vary, but might include collaboration in teaching and the exchange of ideas on new developments. Headmasters will meet for similar purposes.

Headmasters often believe it important to maintain good relations with the community in which their schools are located. Their public relations exercises may be seen as part of a process of neutralizing the environment. Headmasters may wish to avert hostility on the part of certain environmental bodies and, more positively, to persuade these bodies to legitimitize the school and its activities. Thus, headmasters may make a point of joining local associations which have no direct and obvious educational value to the school. In the same way, they may be anxious to maintain friendly relations with local community development associations, the local police and others.

An interesting example of the way in which a school can utilize and, at the same time, attempt to neutralize its environment, comes from the experience of a private school. Boys from the famous Rugby school are reported to be "getting into the nitty-gritty of the town through their involvement with young children, both normal and subnormal, handicapped and disabled young people, the old and the helpless". The boys garden and decorate for old people, "help to coach ESN children at football, introduce a handicapped child to pottery or the piano, or bring immigrant children to Rugby's language labs so that they can improve their English. They go into local primary schools and take over drama for an afternoon, turning children into rabbits and squirrels while they take on the role of the Wizard or Story Teller".[5] The headmaster of the school is reported as saying that the school learns as much as it is able to give and that the contact with the town is valued. At the same time, he is aware of a "degree of reserve" which may exist in a town where the pupils of the boarding school are not local but he hopes, according to the report, that Rugby town will be more understanding of the school as a result of these activities.

The school can also engage with its environment in another way which is not usefully accommodated in the categories of 'utilization' and 'neutralization' of the environment. The example here is of the community school, where an attempt is made to integrate the school into the local community to a much greater extent than normally happens. Noting that the community school has as many different definitions as there are people opening their mouths on the topic, Eric Midwinter says that "most of them tend towards an 'open' as opposed to a 'closed' school, with more intensive usage of plant by the community in evenings and during holidays and usually some pattern of parental participation in school-life". He goes on:

> "The Community School is normally seen as a method of achieving harmony between school and community, but it could go beyond that. As well as providing a means, it could suggest an end. In the EPA (Educational Priority Area) the fundamental need is for communal regeneration and for the resolution of the dreadful social ills that beset the inhabitants.

Eventually, this should mean some form of self-regeneration as the people involved set about solving these problems. The pouring in of palliatives, in resources or services, from outside is not sufficient; indeed, without the active and vital participation of the local inhabitants such interventionist policies lose much of their point. The transference of social and educational problems to the new housing estates emphasizes this. A natural aim, then, for the community school might be the education of children to be the next generation of parents, voters and citizens in the neighbourhood, in the hope that they will conceive of creative responses to the pressing needs of the down-town and other disadvantaged districts".[6]

So far we have discussed the environment almost as though it existed in categories. We have talked about the social background in terms of customs and beliefs; we have referred to the administrative environment and the immediate locale of the schools; and we have discussed the ways in which the school engages with its environment. Of course, these are analytical categories and in reality all of these different aspects of the environment are inextricably intermingled. Additionally, and in consequence of this, these different aspects of the environment are not simply acting upon the school, but are acting upon each other as well. Clearly the customs and beliefs of a society, will influence the government and local authorities, the community in which a school is situated, parents, pressure groups, teachers' unions and other organizations, just as much as they influence the school itself. Just as clearly, the activities of all of these bodies, their impact on the schools and the society to which they belong, will have some sort of effect on the customs and beliefs of that society.

In the same way, pressure groups influence not just the school. The government departments responsible for education are perhaps most in contact with pressure groups.

As we have seen, although schools are directly affected by government departments, through regulations, requests for information, and Her Majesty's Inspectors, the local authorities are also affected. Similarly, these government departments are affected by the activities of the local authorities, who will be submitting plans for new projects, building programmes, and so on. Bodies like the Schools Council clearly have an effect not only, and perhaps not even primarily, on individual schools, but also on local education authorities, government departments, education pressure groups, and the like. The local education authorities will be the targets of pressure groups concerned with changing aspects of school education within their areas, or pressure groups concerned with maintaining the existing system in the face of proposed changes. The teachers' unions have more direct contact with local authorities and government departments than with schools, although the schools may in one sense be most affected by action taken by unions, as in the Teesside dispute.

This dispute occurred in the context of a reorganization of secondary schools into comprehensives. The local authority had proposed to treat all teaching posts as new ones. The existing staff of the schools would have to apply for the 'new' jobs. This arrangement was unacceptable to many of the staff involved, particularly those belonging to the National Association of Schoolmasters, and in retaliation teachers began to work to contract. Subsequently, the authority modified its position and said that teachers would be placed in comparable posts where possible. This was still not acceptable to the union and a large number of teachers were suspended or dismissed. Eventually, the Department of Education and Science (although it was not an employing body) and the Department of Employment set up a committee of inquiry into the dispute. The committee produced a report criticizing both sides in the dispute.

The dispute drew attention to the difficulties for

education authorities and teaching staff, in a situation where schools are being reorganized. Staff are naturally anxious about job security and will be concerned about a situation where they may be effectively dismissed without what they would regard as good reason, such as proof of incompetence. On the other hand, the education authority will want to appoint what they regard as suitable staff to schools whose character is being radically altered. In the meantime, the schools are being affected by a dispute in which they are only indirectly involved. Other examples could be quoted where schools have been affected, perhaps even forced to close down, by 'external' disputes.

[2] Birley, D.; *The education officer and his world,* London, Routledge and Kegan Paul (1970), pp. 19–20.

[3] Hunter, S. Leslie.; *The Scottish Educational System,* Oxford, Pergamon Press (1968), p. 39.

[4] Osborne, G. S.; *Scottish and English Schools,* London, Longmans (1966), p. 33.

[5] *The Guardian,* 9/1/73.

[6] Midwinter, Eric; *Curriculum and the EPA community school,* Liverpool Educational Priority Area Occasional Papers, No. 6, 1970; Reprinted in R. Hooper, (ed), *The Curriculum: Context Design and Development,* Edinburgh, Oliver and Boyd, in association with The Open University Press (1971), p. 484.

CHAPTER 2

The Goals of the School

The deputy headmaster of one school, in answer to the question "What are the goals of this school?", replied "Oh, no, not on a Monday morning." He went on to say that he would have the same difficulty on any other morning. People usually have difficulty in answering such a question in terms which are relevant to what they do in the schools each day. They begin by admitting that what they are going to say is stereotyped, high flown, pompous or, to all intents and purposes, meaningless. "To give the children a good education", "to make the children fit for society", "to give the children the opportunity to develop to the best of their abilities", are typical answers. It is not that these phrases are devoid of meaning, but, apart from the fact that they, or similar ones have been repeated countless times at conferences and meetings, in books, articles and speeches, they do not take us very far. They do not help us to understand what happens in schools.

In a sense these phrases refer to 'givens', or what we might call necessary conditions. We can assume that a school will attempt to give children a good education. If it did not attempt this we would have to consider calling it something else. The questions which these phrases give rise to are much more difficult. What is meant by 'a good education' or 'to the best of their abilities'? That a variety of meanings can be attached to phrases such as these, is one of the reasons why schools differ so much from one another. Most people would subscribe to these phrases, but it is only when people start acting on them that we can see that there is a whole range of other factors at work. It is possible to agree with such a statement and at the same time to disagree whole-heartedly with what a school is actually doing.

If this is the case why should we bother ourselves with the goals of a school? Should we not look simply at the activities which occur in the school? The reason is that goal analysis illuminates the behaviour of the members of the school. We can understand more of what goes on in a school if we know what objectives are being sought. Much of a school's activity is explained (or justified) by the staff, by referring to the goals of the school. Some differences between schools are merely slight differences in method or style of teaching and administration. Other schools are so unlike one another as to reveal fundamental differences of aim and approach.

There are, however, difficulties in trying to talk about the goals of a school. What do we mean by the term 'school' in this context? Some people say that in talking about the goals of a school or any other organization we are attributing characteristics to the organization which should more properly be attributed to an individual or a group of individuals. 'The school' refers to a group of people who are associated with a particular activity which happens to occur regularly in an identifiable building. In other words, the school is a social construct which cannot itself act or think. Actions in the name of the school, will be taken by individuals or groups of individuals.

Another difficulty is that of actually ascertaining what the goals of a school are. If we try asking people who work in the school, there is the difficulty of deciding whom to ask. Should we ask the headmaster and his senior colleagues? Or should we ask everyone who works in the school? If we do the latter, how do we make sense of the conflicting and contradictory statements which we are likely to receive? Even if we were able to do this satisfactorily, would we be any nearer to ascertaining the goals of the school by an analysis of these statements? If we decide instead to observe activity in the school, we are faced with the same difficulties. Whose activity do we observe? All activity? How do we make sense of it? How could we be sure that we would be able to infer the goals from an analysis of the activity? It might be more sensible both to ask what members of the school see as the goals of the school, and to observe activity. There is, however, still the problem of matching what we observed with the stated goals of the school. We have to categorize the activity in some way and decide which categories of activity match which goals. The assumption here would be that all activity would be directed towards the achievement of stated goals. Not only might this assumption not be correct, but the further implicit assumption is that the only goals are stated.

A further difficulty is that not all goals are of the same order. Some will be relatively short-term, others long-term. In addition, some short-term goals may be the basis for longer-term goals. For instance, it may be thought that part of what is necessary to give children a good education (long-term goal) is for them to have an understanding of Archimedes' Principle, or the causes of the First World War (short-term goal). For children to have a good education it may be necessary for them to have an extensive knowledge of English literature, together with some fluency in French and German, and some knowledge of French and German literatures. In this case, three long-term goals contribute to another long-term goal (that of a good education). Another way of putting this is to say that the means to the end of providing a good education are to ensure a knowledge of English, French and German.

It would be helpful in this situation to be able to categorize goals in such a way as to make sense of the activities of a school and the differing statements of goals which we are likely to meet. There is no accepted method of categorizing goals, although there are many which are acceptable. The following analysis, therefore, is presented as one possible way of categorizing goals which may help to resolve some of the difficulties over goal-statements.

In the first place, there is a basic set of aims which are derived from the meaning of the word school. Without these goals the organization would not be a school, it would be some other kind of organization. In other words, these goals form a part of the conditions which have to exist before we can say that the organization is a school. They are the necessary conditions, or conditional goals of the school. Its existence as a school is conditional on its having such goals as "to give the children an education", "to give the children the opportunity to develop to the best of their abilities." Secondly, there are legitimitizing goals. These are concerned with the school's relationship with its environment. For example, one such goal might be to maintain grammar school standards in a comprehensive school. The justification for this might be that it was essential to achieve or keep the respect of the local community. Other goals in this category might be concerned with the school's relationship with its local education authority.

Thirdly, there are official goals, which may be rather more specific than the first two categories. Official goals may include the development of sex education, community involvement, social education, or environmental education. We can distinguish between official goals which are internally generated and official goals which are externally generated. The examples given above may be for instance goals which have been decided upon inside the school. On the other hand when local authorities build and staff schools they may wish to impose a certain style of education and may influence the schools to emphasize certain aspects of education by the facilities which they provide.

Fourthly, there are individual or group goals. There are two types of individual goals which are relevant here.

Individuals have personal aims, such as achieving promotion and earning more money. These would be
personally-oriented goals. They may also have aims which
are organizationally-oriented. These would include goals
or tasks set by organizational superiors, as well as aims
which they may have concerning that part of the activity
of the organization in which they have an interest or for
which they are responsible. A head of department, for
example, might wish to introduce new methods of
teaching or a new syllabus; a headmaster might wish to
improve the administration of the school. Group goals
would include departmental goals and the goals of
'pressure groups' within the school.

A fifth set of goals are a result of the actual
working of the school. We may call them active goals or
operative goals. These can be revealed only by observing
school activity and assessing the time and energy devoted
to the various activities. Community involvement may be
stressed as an official goal of the school but we can
determine whether this is an active goal only by observing
the amount of activity which is devoted to this. In the
same way we can attempt to assess the weight given to
scientific education as opposed to aesthetic education,
intra-curricular as opposed to extra-curricular activities.
Active goals are delimited by legitimitizing goals and will
be influenced by the interaction between the differing and
in part conflicting goals of individuals and groups.

In practice, of course, much of a school's energy will
normally be devoted to the requirements of the external
examination system, although schools differ in the emphasis they place on this. For many headmasters and
teachers, and of course for many parents as well,
schools are in business to put pupils successfully through
the examination system. Some primary schools, for
example, acquire a reputation for a high pass rate at the
11-plus, and some secondary schools are said to present for
external examinations only those pupils who are certain to

pass or who have a good chance of doing so. Conversely, other schools present all pupils for these examinations, and their staffs seem unconcerned about pass rates. Naturally, if teachers are concerned about pass rates, perhaps because the school is new and they want to establish a good academic reputation, or if they want to attract a steady supply of good teachers, this will affect their policy with regard to the examination system.

The point was made earlier that there are difficulties in talking about the goals of a school because strictly speaking 'the school' cannot act or have goals. It is the people who belong to the organization who can do these things. According to this we could presumably talk only about the goals of the headmaster or the goals of a member of staff or group of staff. There are occasions when this would certainly be the best way of describing a situation. If we wanted to make an analysis of the organization of the school, we would want to know what were the goals of the headmaster, distinguishing between his personally-oriented and organizationally-oriented goals. But unless we assume total dominance of the school by its headmaster, this would not be adequate. We would also have to inquire about the goals of the members of staff, again distinguishing between their personally-oriented goals and the goals they were working towards in their work. We could not, of course, assume total unanimity among the staff, or even among small groups of staff. They may subscribe, with varying degrees of conviction, to a number of ideas, but they will react differently to the situations with which they have to cope. Their assessments of situations and, therefore, the actions they take, will differ even though they subscribe to a common goal. In addition, they will interpret that goal in individual ways.

We could arrive, then, at a list of goals, some of which might be legitimitizing goals, affecting the image presented to the environment; others would be official goals, some derived from environmental bodies, others sanctioned by the authority of, at least, the headmaster; and still others would be goals attributable to individuals or groups in the school. In order to arrive at an assessment of active or operative goals, however, we would have to inspect the activity of the school. We could not necessarily attribute active goals to any particular individuals or groups, because they derive from the interactions between the members of the school and are mediated by the structural arrangements within the school. People do not act simply in accordance with ideas and goals which are important to them. The interact with others in the performance of their duties and are influenced by other people's ideas, attitudes and actions. Their behaviour and the attainment of their goals are constrained by structural requirements. In other words, in the performance of organizational activities they have to act in approved and predictable ways. There are occasions, of course, when people act in ways which are not approved, or which are approved by some and disapproved by others, and conflict may occur. In the main, however, behaviour in a school is approved and predictable, in the sense that, on the simplest level, a particular class will be taught a certain subject in a certain room at a prearranged time. The structure of a school provides the framework within which activity occurs and it necessarily constrains this activity, thus producing effects which may not have been looked for by the participants. In this sense organizational activity may be said to be working towards a goal, although it may not be an intentional one.

Goals are affected, then, by structural arrangements within the school, but we should also note that goals themselves influence structural arrangements. Some schools divide their pupils into streams which differ according to their perceived ability. Others place pupils in mixed ability classes, although the pupils may be taught different subjects in classes differentiated according to their ability in that subject. These differing arrangements will reflect the differing goals held in schools, although they will also be a result of the current uncertainty as to how children best learn. Connected with these arrangements are another set of arrangements which determine which pupils are to be taught which subjects, and at what level. For example, pupils may be divided into 'academic' and 'non-academic' at an early stage, the course which they will take depending on their designation. This may mean that those designated 'academic' will take a standard academic course leading to recognized external examinations, whereas those designated 'non-academic' will take a course which does not lead to external academic examinations. The latter pupils may then be encouraged to leave school at the first opportunity. Other schools operate a less rigid system whereby pupils may be allowed to study subjects according to their perceived ability in each subject. Once again, these differing arrangements reflect the goals held in the school and the values on which goals are based.

One of the difficulties in analysing the goals of a school is the great variety of goals which it is possible to identify. For example, a school may be trying to develop a sense of community involvement in its pupils, it may be trying to prepare pupils for university life, trying to improve its external examination pass rate, trying to involve parents in the life of the school, trying to cut down on truancy, or trying to encourage as many pupils as possible to stay on past the statutory leaving age. Different schools put emphasis on different goals. One school may be attempting to develop a social education programme and may put a great deal of time and effort on the part of its senior staff into this objective. Another school may decide that the difficulties in this area are too great and decide to wait and see what examples are produced from which it can learn.

Schools also differ in the energy they put into activity unconcerned with examinations or the formal curriculum. Leisure-time activities are an example. As well as the usual extra-curricular activities which normally take place after school closes or during the lunch hour, some schools set aside time during the weekly time-table when pupils are given the opportunity of learning activities which would normally take place out of school. The justification for this may be that pupils need to be equipped for the life of increased leisure time which some people think they will almost certainly lead. Pastoral guidance must also be included here. It is often said that schools have always been concerned with more than simply teaching their pupils how to read and write, or how to analyse a poem to the satisfaction of the external examiners, or to be able to state Archimedes' Principle and Boyle's Law. Headmasters and other teachers in small schools often know all the pupils in their schools by name and might often know something about the family background of the pupils. Register teachers would perhaps know the pupils best of all as they see them every day during the school session. However, register teachers do not all take the same interest in their pupils and, particularly with the growth of large schools, it was felt that headmasters had neither the time nor the energy to be able to know their pupils as well as they might wish and certainly did not have the time to attend to the difficulties of all the pupils who might in some way be having trouble. This will be discussed in more detail in a later chapter.

The goals of a school will develop in part out of the interaction between the school and its environment. The importance of the environment for the school has already been discussed. Account has to be taken at the broadest level of what is acceptable in the wider society in which the school is situated. Most schools are owned and maintained by local authorities which can, through their education committees and professional administrative staff, exercise considerable influence on the schools. This influence may be direct, as in the case of a decision to change to a system of comprehensive education, or a decision to introduce a new staffing structure; or it may be indirect as in the case of a change in the catchment area of the school. In the case of a change to comprehensive education, or even with a change in catchment area, the staff of the schools may be forced to change or re-interpret their goals because of the different kinds of pupils they may be receiving. In addition, members of the Inspectorate who visit schools will influence what schools are trying to achieve and the methods they employ. As we have noted in the chapter on environment, the external examination boards exercise considerable influence on what is taught in schools, and the system of external examina-tions and the importance attached to them means that teachers' freedom is limited in terms of subjects taught and methods employed. Schools will also be influenced by the continuing educational debate carried on in newspapers, journals and books. Headmasters and teachers visit each other to find out what is going on in other schools, and to some extent their friends will be drawn from the teaching profession. Committees and working parties proliferate—the goals of a school will be set not in isolation, but in the context of such interaction.

In the context of a debate on teacher training, A. S. Neill, in a letter to a newspaper, wrote that "Teachers should not be trained to teach; they should be trained to deal mainly with the emotional side of their pupils, their character, their happiness. How many teachers know what to do with a young thief or destroyer?" He went on to say that "'O' and 'A' levels are no test of ability, but, if we must have them, why not make them fit in with the real interests of the young? I can suggest additional subjects that would attract youth . . . an 'O' level in football, tennis, stamp-collecting, photography, horsemanship, even pop music, ecology. . . . Alas, one cannot teach anything of im-portance. Maths, yes, but not how to love, to be charit-able, how to be sincere."[7]

Eric Midwinter has written that even if we are not

prepared to abandon examinations, we could make them worthwhile in terms both of interest and day-to-day use. "Let us, at least, have interesting and useful 'O' levels and CSEs, ones that take into account that adolescents become householders, workers, voters, leisure-pursuers, consumers, lovers, and parents—and also that they are still adolescents. So a list of examination subjects might read: community affairs, leisure pursuits, consumer studies, marriage and parenthood, home and child management, domestic economics, transition to work, local politics—all negotiated with practical activity where feasible, and imaginative challenge. Then, as well as the normal academic subjects and beyond the aesthetic pursuits like literature, art and music, there could be a range of themes such as pop culture, football appreciation, television, fashion, and so forth." He asserts that this is far from being anti-intellectual. "It could well be considerably more intellectually and creatively stimulating than some of the dull, wan, 'academic' pap that leaves our secondary children too often restless and bored."[8]

Jo Grimond has been reported as saying that he thought it scandalous that, at the end of their period in school, there were many practical skills which children had not acquired. Too many children left school unable to speak a foreign language, unable to understand an ordinary balance sheet, unable to mend a car, or to carry out ordinary household repairs.[9]

Another view was put by H. G. Judge. Voicing the thoughts of many teachers, he said that it was time to reassert the priority of intellectual and academic aims within the schools, and to begin to redress the balance away from social towards academic objectives.[10] Many people are concerned that the growth of comprehensive schools and the spread of 'progressive' ideas about what children should be taught and the methods to be employed, will lead to a decline in academic standards.

Clearly, there is a good deal of disagreement as to what

schools should be trying to do. Universities, colleges, employers and parents all have a stake in what happens in schools, as well as the children themselves, who are most affected and have the least say. What happens in schools is important because children's experiences in school are influential in teaching them certain types of behaviour and in exposing them to certain attitudes. In other words, teaching involves not only the transmission of knowledge, but also value-laden behaviour.

Conflict may arise as a result of this. A school's goals, or the values which are inherent in those goals and in the way activity is structured in the school, may conflict with those of the parents of at least some of the pupils. A school may, for example, attach great importance to punctuality and tidiness. It can easily be seen why. If children are not punctual in arriving at classes, teaching may be interrupted and disrupted, so that one of the main goals of the school is made more difficult, given that the way most schools attempt to achieve the goal of imparting a body of knowledge is by means of a strict timetable which involves groups of people moving from place to place at prearranged times. On the other hand a child's parents may not attach great importance to punctuality, preferring to emphasize other values. Similarly with tidiness. In a school of a thousand or more pupils it is relatively easy to understand the school's concern that litter should not be dropped and that materials should be cleared away properly after use, ready for the next group. In the context of the home, however, these issues may appear to some people to be of minor importance.

Should a school's values override that of parents? This is clearly an important question. One can see some justification for the view that it may be as well for children to learn the value of punctuality and tidiness to the society in which they live, and that school may be a good place to do this. On the other hand, what other values is the school emphasizing? Which values is it neglecting? Who is involved in selecting these values? What are the criteria for selecting some and neglecting others? Are teachers better equipped to educate children than the parents of those children, except in carefully defined areas of knowledge, such as mathematics, modern languages and science? If so, what is it in their education, training and experience which makes them better equipped?

As far as the subjects usually taught in school are concerned, there is for the most part an established body of knowledge which can be defined and in which people can be regarded as expert. There may be a great deal of argument within each of these fields as to what should be included in the school curriculum, or concerning the best methods of teaching these subjects, but as far as the non-experts are concerned, although they may have opinions as to the results obtained by the experts and may quite properly voice these opinions, nevertheless they are for the most part content to leave decisions in these areas to those whom they regard as expert. Concerning moral or social education, however, there is no such established body of knowledge or group of recognized experts. There may be almost as many definitions of proper behaviour as there are people. Certainly, there are no agreed ways. Yet schools establish rigid definitions of proper behaviour and punish pupils for deviating from them. For example, many schools still insist that pupils address staff members as 'sir' or 'miss'. Clearly this is no longer the accepted mode of address to adults outside schools.

And schools instil the habit, or attempt to, of obedience to orders, particularly those given by senior teachers. It could be argued that this is not the best way of training children to think for themselves, and since habits learned early in life are often difficult to break, of training adults to think for themselves. Again, one can appreciate the difficulty of those who are in charge of schools. They have to ensure that pupils and staff are in certain places at the right times, otherwise they would not be able to do what they see as their duty. Nevertheless, if children are to be taught obedience, punctuality and tidiness in formal social education programmes as well as through participating in the everyday life of the school, then it could be argued that there are other values which are at least as worthy of inclusion, if not more so. The problem then becomes one of ensuring their inclusion.

Parents have been kept traditionally rigidly separate from the life of the school, except under carefully controlled conditions. In some areas at least, the headmaster of a school must give his consent before a parent-teacher association may be formed. Consequently, many schools have no such association. Headmasters are often suspicious of the influence of parents acting in concert. Local authority notices may be seen in schools forbidding parents to approach any teacher without first obtaining the permission of the headmaster. There may be good reasons for such a notice. It may interfere with the running of the school to have parents wandering about uninvited. There is no doubt, however, that these notices are often seen as indicative of the lowly place which parents occupy in the educational system.

We can legitimately question this state of affairs. The aims that teachers are attempting to achieve are clearly important not simply for teachers, but also for the children and their parents. In which case, should the goals of a school be more actively influenced by parents? How would this influence be best exercised? And in what way would the goals of a school, and the values emphasized in the school, be different if parents were more closely involved?

[7] Letter in *The Guardian*, 28/1/72.
[8] Article in *The Guardian*, 18/4/72.
[9] Reported in *The Scottish Educational Journal*, Vol. 54, No. 43, 3/12/71.
[10] Reported in *The Guardian*, 6/1/73.

CHAPTER 3

School Structure

When people talk about the structure of an organization they are usually referring to the formal pattern of jobs and job titles which exist independently of the persons who actually fill them. It may be helpful to look at the formal staff structure of two hypothetical schools. Each school, of course, has a headmaster. In the first, an English school, there is a deputy headmaster who deputizes for the head as necessary and who is in charge of the general day-to-day running of the school. He is responsible for the discipline of boys in the school, and for the supervision of male student-teachers in conjunction with heads of departments. A senior mistress is responsible for the discipline of girls and supervise female student-teachers. She also co-ordinates house matters, and has a particular responsibility for social functions in the school. She has a share of general administrative jobs. There are three heads of school. The head of upper school is in charge of sixth-form studies, careers guidance in the sixth-form, links with colleges, universities and firms, and parental contacts. The head of middle school has a particular responsibility for careers guidance and work experience projects, and has to allocate pupils to courses. The head of lower school is responsible for liaison with local primary schools, visits pupils at these schools and organizes meetings of their parents to tell them about the secondary school. He is in charge of the allocation of new pupils to classes and house groups and he is also concerned with the junior school curriculum.

In addition there are the heads of subject departments

AN ENGLISH SCHOOL

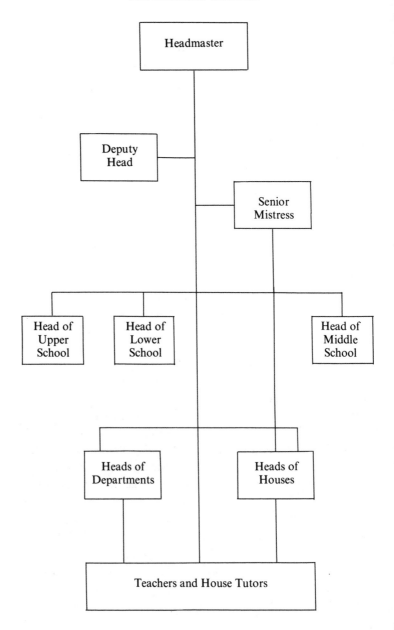

A SCOTTISH SCHOOL

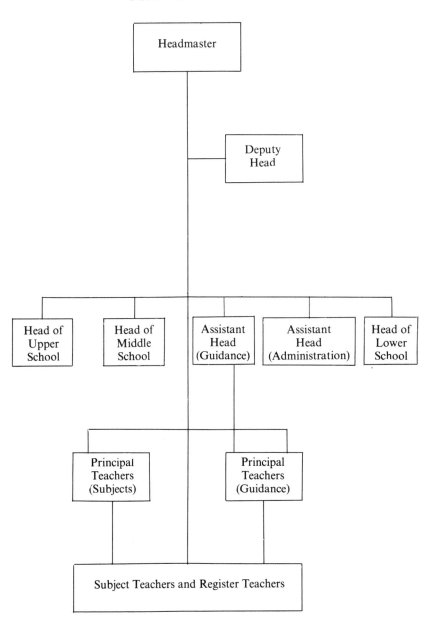

who are responsible for the teaching of their subjects, and the house staff who are responsible for the welfare of the children in their houses and contacts with parents. House tutors have charge of individual form groups and are responsible to the head of each house for the pastoral care of these groups. They are responsible to the heads of school for the academic progress of the form. Subject teachers are, of course, responsible to their heads of department for the teaching of· their classes and for discipline in those classes.

In the second school, a Scottish one, the duties of the deputy head are similar to those of his English counter-part—he deputizes when necessary and is responsible for the day-to-day running of the school. There are five assistant headmasters in the school and three of them act as heads of school. The head of upper school is responsible for supervision of the curriculum and careers guidance in the fifth and sixth, providing information on universities and colleges, and writing references for pupils going on to higher education. The head of middle school's responsibility covers the curriculum in the third and fourth years, with particular reference to developing suitable curricula for those who will be leaving at the statutory leaving age. He also arranges courses for pupils and careers programmes. The head of lower school is in charge of liaison with primary schools, arranges visits for the new intake and meetings for their parents, allocates pupils to courses and houses, and has a responsibility for supervising the curriculum in the first two years. The heads of school are responsible for discipline in their respective year groupings. It happens that the head of lower school is a woman and so she has been asked by the headmaster to look after the discipline of the girls in the school. She has also been asked by him to take part in official functions in the school, acting as hostess when the school has visitors. Of the two other assistant headmasters, one is concerned with administration and has general administrative duties, working with the deputy head and the headmaster; the other has overall charge of the guidance or house system.

The principal teachers (heads of departments) are in charge of the teaching in their subjects and subject teachers are responsible to them for class teaching and class discipline. There are also principal teachers (guidance), otherwise called senior housemasters (or senior housemistresses), who are responsible for the welfare of the children allocated to their houses. They may have one or two assistants each. The children are attached to register classes and the register teachers are responsible to the senior house staff for attendance and some aspects of pastoral care.

This, then, is the formal structure of these organizations. An organization chart for each school is shown on pp 48, 49. It is useful to be acquainted with the organization chart of a particular organization when we first have dealings with it. It helps to clarify the matter of whom we may want to talk to in the first instance. But it does not tell the whole story. The misleading nature of the formal chart or plan can be illustrated easily. The deputy headmaster of a school is formally the second most powerful person in the school. In practice he may be kept away from all important decisions in the school. A head of a teaching department, on the other hand, who may formally be two or three steps down the hierarchy, may have the ear of the headmaster and wield an influence out of all proportion to his formal status.

Formal structure is only one aspect of what is meant here by 'structure.' Structure can be taken to refer to the established pattern of relationships in an organization. This is not to say that the pattern will remain unchanged. Relationships are changing all the time. New people may be coming into the organization, bringing new ideas, habits and assumptions, others will be leaving. Contacts with the world outside the organization will also affect the pattern of relationships, and change outside the school will have an effect inside. Similarly, ideas will change about what the organization ought to be doing (in other words, about the goals of the organization), and about the proper methods of doing it. This again will affect relationships within the organization. Even without the stimulus of an influx of new people, the pattern will change as ideas change and as people alter their attitudes and assumptions about other people in the organization. New estimates will be made of people's abilities as they tackle new or different tasks. Nevertheless, for our purposes we may assume that at any given time there will exist a particular pattern of relationships.

These relationships will be of varying kinds. In any school there are friendship relations, colleague relationships, hostility relationships, relationships where one person gives advice to another, relationships where one person gives orders to another. These will of course overlap, making the picture even more complex. Relationships between staff will be radically different from relationships between staff and pupils. Relationships between pupils will be different again. Even in the relationships between staff and pupils there will be variations. A register teacher will probably have a different, and perhaps closer, relationship with his class than will the head of a subject department who does not teach that class but who is responsible for the class's progress in his subject. The class's relationship with the headmaster will possibly be different again, as will their relationship with the member of staff who is responsible for their welfare.

In different organizations different patterns of relationships will exist. This may be particularly so if the organizations are engaged in widely differing activities. Even where the organizations are engaged in the same activity, however, different structures or patterns of relationships are apparent, as in the case of our two hypothetical examples of schools which may be said to be engaged in broadly the same activity. We can say further that even where two schools, for example, are set up with exactly the same formal structure the patterns of relationships may vary greatly. To know about structure we need to know how the organization functions in practice. We need to know how individuals relate to each other and how they perceive the organization. We must know the rules and procedures in force within the organization, what arrangements are used for regular activities, what policies are adopted and acted upon. Only then will it be possible for us to arrive at a clear understanding of the structure of the organization. Of course, it would be almost impossible to have a complete picture of the structure, in the sense of being acquainted with all relationships in the organization. What we can attempt to do, however, is to identify people and relationships which have important consequences for the activity of the organization.

School organization has certain features which are normally attributed to bureaucracies. In a bureaucracy, staff positions are organized into a hierarchy, with people lower down the hierarchy reporting to those higher up; there is a marked degree of differentiation between tasks with specialist personnel performing them; and the activity of the organization is carried out according to specific rules and procedures. The hierarchical principle is evident from the organization charts on pp 48, 49. The headmaster has overall responsibility for all activity in the school, the heads of departments are responsible to him for the teaching in their departments, and the individual teachers are responsible to their heads of departments for the teaching of their classes. However, members of staff do not simply report to their immediate superiors in the school hierarchy. They have a variety of relationships with other members of staff. A teacher may be, for example, a register teacher and in some way responsible to another member of staff (perhaps a housemaster or yearmaster) for the welfare and behaviour of that class. He may have to report continued absence or suspected truancy to another member of staff. He will probably be a teacher in a subject department responsible to his head of department for the teaching and progress of his classes in that subject. The deputy head or some other person may call upon him to take a class in place of an absent teacher. He may be asked to report on a pupil in one of his classes by a member of the guidance staff if the matter concerns the pupil's behaviour, or by some other member of staff if the matter concerns the pupil's overall academic progress.

One of the reasons why a teacher may be involved in so many relationships is because of increased specialization in schools. In small schools in the past (and even today in some areas) the headmaster alone was responsible for the welfare and behaviour, attendance and academic progress of his pupils and perhaps also for the everyday teaching in the school. In the first place, however, knowledge has become more specialized so that we have experts in chemistry, for example, who would claim at most only a passing acquaintance with modern languages. In the second place, the number of pupils in schools has grown so that more than one teacher of chemistry may be needed. In this way the system of teaching departments with one person as head of each department has grown up. Similarly, the headmaster of a large school would find it difficult to deal with all the everyday administrative problems himself. The number of teachers appointed to deal with matters which at one time would have been dealt with by the headmaster (or perhaps not done at all) has also expanded. Most schools have a deputy headmaster who is required not merely to deputize if the headmaster is ill or away from the school, but also to perform other tasks, such as examination arrangements or finding replacements for absentee teachers. In addition, as the feeling became widespread that the headmaster of a large school could not give the amount of attention to individual pupils which was thought necessary, teachers or other persons have been appointed and specifically charged with looking after the personal welfare of a number of pupils. Specialization may emerge or conscious decisions may be taken about it. We may suppose that the system of specialized subject teaching has emerged over the years, as knowledge has increased and new subjects have been added to the curriculum. Subject departments gradually split away from each other as people began to specialize in new areas of knowledge. On the other hand, in the case of the recent establishment of posts of assistant headmasters in Scottish schools, decisions had to be taken as to the kind of activities in which each assistant headmaster would specialize.

Specialization in activity and specialization of knowledge often lead to specialization in authority. Clearly, those who specialize in the teaching of French have a much better chance of becoming experts at it than those who do not. When we say that someone is an expert we are acknowledging that he is an authority on some activity or in some area of knowledge. We are entitled to expect that the heads of subject departments in a school will be experts in their subject, certainly in comparison with most of the other people they are likely to have dealings within the school. Their authority in their subjects is likely to be acknowledged by their colleagues, unless for some reason their colleagues feel that they are incompetent and unworthy of the status of expert. Apart from their authority based on knowledge, heads of departments have another kind of authority based on their position in the hierarchy. Because of this, the approval of a head of department will be necessary before certain kinds of activity can occur in his department. New schemes of work and new methods of teaching, for example, will depend to some extent on the approval of heads of departments.

On the pastoral side of the school's activity, the persons

in charge of houses will also have an authority based on their position in the hierarchy, which may be equal to that of the heads of departments. They may be paid the same money and have the same formal status as the heads of departments. As far as authority based on knowledge is concerned, however, the situation may be quite different, because their colleagues in the school may not acknowledge that the heads of houses have expert knowledge. They may think that form teachers or register teachers do an adequate job of keeping an eye on pupils and that a house or some other kind of guidance structure is unnecessary. Another aspect of this situation is that whereas the system of subject departments has existed for a good many years, it is only relatively recently that guidance structures have been set up. Heads of departments, therefore, have an element of traditional authority which house staff do not possess. Of course, housemasters may develop a personal authority of their own. Individuals who are seen to do a competent job within the school and who manage to maintain good relationships with heads of departments and others, may be accorded a status which is not derived from their hierarchical position. These individuals may be noted as exceptions. What may develop from this is that, as guidance staff gain competence and acquire their own specialized skills, they may be accorded expert status by their colleagues in the school. Other teachers may come to recognize that the guidance staff know more than they do about the problems of guidance, and have more experience in treating such problems. The authority which the guidance staff have by virtue of their place in the hierarchy will then be bolstered by an authority based on their knowledge and experience. Additionally, they may acquire a degree of traditional authority as it becomes accepted that they and their successors are a permanent feature of schools.

Specialization and the increase in size of schools have led to a structural complexity. We now have large schools, each with a number of teaching departments, together with pastoral guidance staff, and where teachers may be responsible to different people for a variety of activities. The setting up of certain kinds of pastoral guidance systems, where those concerned with pastoral guidance are also teaching for a part of their time, can also lead to structural complexity. Heads of houses in this case will also be members of subject departments. Although they may be equal in formal status with the heads of departments they must theoretically accept direction from them on academic matters. Similarly, in some schools at least, all staff are attached to houses and are theoretically subordinate to the house staff in that capacity. There are clearly possibilities of conflict here. If the heads of departments do not acknowledge the expert authority of the heads of houses they may resent being placed in a position subordinate to them. They may consequently refuse (although perhaps not explicitly) to co-operate.

As far as their own departments are concerned, they may be anxious that their departments' teaching, for which they are responsible, will not be done properly by people who have other major responsibilities. Perhaps it is in the nature of things that, although a housemaster may have allocated to him extra time in which to perform his non-teaching duties, not all of his business can be conducted during this extra time. Pupils may have to be seen urgently, parents may arrive at the school without appointments but nevertheless with urgent business. This sort of contingency may mean that a housemaster is late for his classes or that his teaching is interrupted. A head of department may very properly be concerned about this, particularly if it happens repeatedly. It is quite possible that for some guidance staff, their non-teaching duties will assume a much greater importance than their teaching. Perhaps it is inevitable that we will devote more energy and attention to activities which are under our direct control than to those activities which are under the control of others. Of course, people cope with this sort of situation in different ways and some guidance staff are better able to reconcile the two activities in ways which are acceptable to their heads of department, and which nevertheless mean that they are performing their guidance duties to their own satisfaction.

The other characteristic of bureaucracy which was mentioned earlier is that activity is governed by rules. It is here that we come closest to the popular use of the word 'bureaucracy' as referring to unnecessary restrictions and 'red tape.' Headmasters, of course, have long emphasized the rules of procedure. Not very long ago the headmaster of one school issued written instructions to his staff to the effect that classes should remain seated until the bell rings; that staff were authorized to leave their classes one minute (emphasized) early if they were on, for example, cloakroom duty, provided that the pupils had been lined up for dismissal and left with appropriate instructions; that teachers' records of work should be sent to him on a particular day each month; that class tests as well as termly examinations should be held on dates specified by him.

At another school, the headmaster sent a notice to the staff at the beginning of the school year saying among other things that punctuality at all times was essential, that it was "out of order" to send two pupils on a simple errand and that "discretion should be exercised" in the choice of pupil, that "only for very justifiable reasons" might teachers leave their rooms during teaching periods, that it was the duty of every teacher to take to task pupils for "slovenly, bad or incorrect speech", for "improper, untidy or dirty clothing and for lack of personal cleanliness", and that only with the headmaster's "express approval" could the telephone be used for private purposes during class periods.

The staff may regard rules such as these as conflicting with their professionalism as teachers, and as encroaching upon areas which they would regard as properly within their discretion. They may see these rules, therefore, as unnecessarily restrictive. From the headmaster's point of view, he has the safety of the pupils to consider as well as their educational well-being. He may be held responsible if accidents occur in his school and if examination results are not up to expectations. He also has to bear in mind the reaction of the local community to the language and behaviour of the pupils. This kind of pressure may lead him to attempt to exert control over as many activities as possible in order to avert undesirable occurrences. Equally, those aspects of school life which in relative terms he emphasizes and neglects will reflect his own outlook on life, as well as his own capacity as a headmaster.

These two examples point to a basic conflict between professional authority and administrative authority. Professional authority is based on knowledge. The professional acts in a particular way because he thinks that to the best of his knowledge it is the right way to act. The administrator, on the other hand, acts in a particular way because it is in line with rules and regulations and has been approved by his superior. The situation is a little more complex in schools because the administrators are themselves professionals, and, therefore, share the professional norms of teachers, although they may be more oriented than teachers to organizational as opposed to professional requirements. Furthermore, teachers are supervised to a greater extent than most other professionals. Their work is strictly timetabled, their duties are specified by headmasters or heads of departments, they have to report on their work at regular intervals, headmasters and department heads may drop in to classrooms to check on a teacher's ability to handle a particular class, and, of course, examinations check not only on pupil learning, but also on teacher performance.

How do schools arrive at their particular structures? What are the factors involved in determining structure?

Environmental influences will again be important here. For instance, the available models in other organizations, and particularly in other schools are bound to influence the choice of formal structure. In addition, certain outside bodies play a critical role in the establishment of the formal structure of a school. The government departments responsible for education at the national level and the local education authorities have an influence on what each individual school looks like, through regulations, directions or advice.

There is a large area, however, which is left to the discretion of the headmaster. This 'discretionary structure' is one of the features which distinguish schools from one another. Although the headmaster is an important figure in the decisions which lead to the establishment of each school's discretionary structure, it would be misleading to suppose that in reality it is solely the discretion of the headmaster that is important. This may be the case but one could not make this judgement for any individual school without looking at the history of the school and the relevant relationships within the school. In practice, most headmasters rely for advice on, at least, some of their senior staff and decisions often emerge from discussion in a way which makes it difficult to ascertain whose voices were most influential.

Other factors are also important. For example, the goals of the school. What the staff are aiming at will be influential in determining how they set about achieving it. Connected with this is the question of how they define the problem which has to be overcome. If they think of children as divisible into 'learners' and non-learners', 'academic' and 'non-academic', or some such label, they may set up a different structure than if they think of children as willing to learn, but with different aptitudes and abilities which are difficult to fathom and which require that each child should be treated individually as far as possible.

Finally, the individual situation of the school will be a determining factor. There are two aspects to this situation. On the one hand, there is the location of the school, which affects the problems the staff are faced with. A grammar school situated in a middle-class area will face a quite different problem from a comprehensive school situated in a slum area. However, as we have said, the way in which they define the problem will determine the structure which is set up to deal with it. This depends in part on the people who work in the school and this constitutes the second aspect of the situation. People have different experiences, abilities, knowledge and enthusiasms, and all these factors will affect the ways in which they relate to each other, the kinds of discretionary structure which are set up, and the ways in which they make the formal structure of the school work.

Discretionary structure may be taken to refer to the structure of staff committees and pupil organization. For example, meetings of heads of departments will usually be held at fairly frequent intervals. Meetings of house staff or other guidance staff will also occur. The frequency of these meetings, the matters discussed and the person chairing the meetings will all vary from school to school. The same applies to meetings of the whole staff. Some headmasters have a particular dislike of this last type of meeting and call them as infrequently as possible. Finance committees may also exist, although some headmasters take all finance decisions themselves, or with one or two senior staff. The composition of these committees varies. In some schools only senior staff may be invited to attend, whereas in others junior staff and perhaps some pupils may sit on the committees. The powers and influence of these committees again vary. Committees which deal with finance, for instance, may also have a wider remit, such as deciding on some of the activities which occur in the school, or consideration of school rules. There may be committees dealing with staff social events, a variety of interdepartmental committees, and committees dealing with matters such as the school concert or the school's field centre. In larger schools there may be some form of 'cabinet' meeting, or 'board of studies'. In the English school referred to at the beginning of the chapter, this meeting would comprise the headmaster, the deputy head, the senior mistress and the three heads of school. In the Scottish school, the meeting would comprise the headmaster, the deputy head and the five assistant headmasters.

As far as pupil organization is concerned, one of the peculiarities of school structure not under the control of the headmaster and his staff is the system of grouping pupils according to age. Pupils come to the school and, generally speaking, move through the school, as they reach certain ages. Nevertheless, within this overall system there is scope for wide variation. Pupils will be allocated to form or registration groups, which, in the first one or two years, may be identical to teaching groups. They are often streamed according to assessments made of their ability in the primary schools, although these assessments may be altered in the light of their performance in the secondary school. These streamed groups may form the basis of both registration and teaching groups. Alternatively, pupils may be allocated to groups of mixed ability, perhaps only for registration, in which case they will be reorganized into relatively homogeneous ability groups for teaching purposes, or the mixed ability groups may be retained as teaching groups for the first one or two years. These registration classes may be composed of pupils of the same house if the school has a house system based on registration classes, or they may be mixed. There may be a system of tutor groups for the purposes of 'social education' lessons (or discussions), which may be identical with registration classes, or perhaps made up of pupils of different ages and abilities. Schools also differ in the opportunities which are given to pupils to study particular subjects or courses. Some schools decide between pupils on the basis that some of them are academic pupils and will, therefore, take an academic course, others who are not academic will take a non-academic course. Others decide on the basis of the pupil's ability in a particular subject what level of teaching he will get in that subject.

These and similar decisions will be taken in the name of educational criteria and criteria related to the techniques of teaching. It may be considered that at least some of these—those related to the techniques of teaching, for example—should be left to those who are experts in the field, in other words to the teachers. However, since there is such wide disagreement in the field which shows itself in the variety of practices to be found in schools, this may indicate that there are other factors at work. These other factors would include the specific situation of individual schools and their difficulties in terms of availability of teachers and resources. Certainly, these considerations are important, but again schools with similar difficulties or advantages differ. The key to the differences may be found in the goals of the school and the moral assumptions of the people who work in it. In other words, what the staff think they are trying to do, what they would like to do, and what they think worthwhile will, in effect, determine the structures which are set up and, therefore, which children will have access to different resources and different kinds of teaching.

Of course, the disagreement between teachers and the wide variety of practices in schools could also mean simply that the best way of teaching and organizing pupils has not yet been found or agreed upon. Implicit in the argument about the best way of teaching children are moral assumptions about what particular children ought to learn and the acceptable methods of teaching them. Is it right that some children in a school should not be given the option of learning French because they are not considered able enough? If they are going to find it difficult, surely that is an argument for allocating more resources to them in order to overcome their difficulties. An objection to this, of course, is that it means taking resources away from abler pupils, from those who are good at French. This may be true. But the assumption here is that the resources would be better spent on those who are good at it, and this is a moral assumption about the relative worth of different children. It is no answer to say that it is a more efficient use of resources to concentrate on the more able pupils. It is certainly not very efficient for the less able. Decisions about efficiency must rest on decisions about what is right and wrong. If this were not the case, we would not allocate so much of our resources on the old, the incurably sick and the handicapped. It would be much more efficient to kill them off and apply the resources to the more productive members of society, but it would be morally wrong.

It may be that one decides, given limited resources, that it is more worthwhile to allocate French teachers to the more able pupils, on the grounds that it is better to make sure that some pupils are very good at French, than to try to teach them all. At least the moral assumption—more worthwhile—is then explicit, and there is less danger of it being confused with technical matters, such as the difficulties of teaching different types of children.

Moral assumptions are also evident in the debate about acceptable teaching methods. For example, sleep learning, subliminal suggestion and hypnosis are all techniques about which there is grave disquiet. They may be effective in getting people to learn but are unacceptable for other, moral reasons. Similarly, there is a controversy as to whether corporal punishment has a part to play in schools. Some teachers consider it essential and believe that if the fear of corporal punishment is removed some children would get out of hand to such a degree that teaching would be made extremely difficult, if not impossible. Others feel that it is wrong to strike children. Either way there

are assumptions about the correct way to treat children.
In some schools children who have arrived at the minimum leaving age may be encouraged to leave whether they wish to or not. The implication is that they have nothing to learn or that the school cannot teach them anything. Some people would think that this entails a narrow view of education in terms of subjects and examination results, and that it implies that interaction with educated adults has nothing to teach these children and will have no effect on them. They might say that for various reasons these children are much more difficult to teach and that, therefore, much more time ought to be spent on them. The opposing view would state that time should not be wasted on such children and that the school's energies should be concentrated on those who will learn and who will be useful members of society. Again moral assumptions about the relative worth of different human beings are implicit in both views.

Ways of dealing with pupils and ways of perceiving them, and hence ways of rewarding or punishing them, will be underpinned by moral assumptions. For example, pupils who break school rules and who are 'disruptive' may be seen as analogous to law-breakers and criminals in the wider society. An alternative view would see them as young people who have not understood the moral basis of rules, which are meant to regulate actions which affect other people. People who hold this view might also want to look at the moral worth of the rules which are being broken. In this context it is clear that many school rules are derived from the opinions and outlooks of the headmaster and his staff and might not stand the test of exposure to a wider audience.

The reason for this is that goals and assumptions on which structural arrangements are based may often be matters of contention. If this is the case, it raises the question of the extent to which structural arrangements should be subject to some form of external control.

E

CHAPTER 4

Influences on Behaviour

People in organizations act in broadly predictable ways. This is what working in an organization means. Their behaviour is constrained by a structure in an attempt to produce activities which will lead to the achievement of desired goals. Of course, this is a very simplified view of what happens. As we have seen, different kinds of goals are pursued in schools. People's behaviour is directed not only towards the achievement of the official goals of the school, but also to their own personal goals or the goals of the groups to which they belong. Their own ideas and values will affect the way they interpret those official goals or attempt to modify them. We can also say that structure affects people's behaviour in different ways. The formal structure lays down certain behavioural requirements, but the actual relationships which exist determine how the formal structure works and the effects it has on people's behaviour.

One of the ways in which structure constrains behaviour is through the roles which people play in the organization. If a person is appointed to teach French in a school, or to put it another way, if that person is assigned to the position of teacher of French, we can be certain that that person will teach French. Furthermore, he or she will teach French to certain children and at certain times decided by other people, such as his or her head of department, the headmaster of the school and the deputy head. We can say these things because we know some of the expectations attached to the position, in other words, we know something of the role of teacher. We know that the role involves accepting direction from other people more senior in the hierarchy, on matters concerning the kind of pupils the teacher will teach and the times and places at which the teaching will be done. All of this will be applicable to most teachers in most schools so that, wherever a teacher goes to teach, he knows that there will be some things certain to be expected of him. Equally, in each school in which the teacher works, there will be other and different things expected of him. His relationships with heads of departments and headmasters will differ from school to school. His relationships with other people will also vary.

They will vary because, although each role may be made up of a set of fairly general expectations (held by other people) as to what the person holding the position will do, that person will also have to interpret those expectations and act on them in the way he thinks best according to those interpretations. The headmaster will interpret his role in a way consistent with his beliefs and experience, and the way in which he interprets his role will affect other people's roles. In other words, his expectations of others will be to some extent personal and individual. The teacher of French has to cope, therefore, not only with a set of generalized expectations concerning his behaviour, but also with the headmaster's interpretations of those generalized expectations, together with particular expectations which the head may have. The teacher in turn interprets the head's expectations and will also bring with him from his own beliefs and experience another set of individual expectations. The picture of inter-locking and interacting expectations is further complicated once we include the expectations and interpretations of other people such as heads of departments and deputy heads.

Role expectations are derived from a variety of sources. There are certain generalized expectations about the behaviour of teachers which are held in the wider society.

Government regulations and the policies and regulations of local authorities will also produce expectations. However, the policies and procedures of the school, school traditions, and ideas and beliefs concerning the goals of the school are also important. This is another reason why all schools are different and why people who are doing what is nominally the same job may, in different schools, become concerned with different activities. Further expectations about a teacher's behaviour will arise from views held by other people in similar positions and by people whose activities are in some way affected by the behaviour of the teacher. Almost all the other staff in the school must be included here, as well as the pupils. They will all have views as to what is expected of a teacher, although their views will, of course, differ and they may be concerned with different aspects of the teacher's role. The house staff will be concerned with the teacher's knowledge of individual pupils and the way in which he or she contributes to those pupils' welfare. The teacher's head of department, on the other hand, will be concerned primarily with the way the teacher performs his teaching duties. The headmaster may be concerned with the teacher's overall professional conduct.

Role expectations differ in intensity. It is against the law for a teacher to have sexual intercourse with an under-age schoolgirl. There is nothing illegal, on the other hand, in his doing so with a schoolgirl over the age of sixteen. It would, however, be unacceptable to most of his colleagues, precisely because the girl was a schoolgirl. This would be much more evident if the girl was a pupil at his school. In this case, the teacher would possibly be dismissed or asked to resign. Similarly, it is acceptable, though not required, for a teacher to interest himself in the school's extra-curricular activities. It may even be an extra recommendation in his favour if he is applying for a promoted post. And, of course, a teacher is required to prepare and conduct his lessons to the satisfaction of his head of department and the headmaster and to make sure that other classes are not disturbed by noise during the course of these lessons.

Views and expectations held by different people will not all be of equal weight. For the headmaster the policies of the local education authority and the views of the chief education officer may be of great importance, whereas for unpromoted members of staff they may be quite remote and unknown. For these latter people the views and policies of the headmaster may be of much greater importance. The views of their heads of department, of course, affect what they do from day to day.

Role expectations will not necessarily be clear or well understood. A teacher may discover that he has done something contrary to the expectation of his behaviour held by others only when he receives a reprimand or word of warning from his headmaster, or when he is criticized or made fun of by his colleagues in the staff room. Again there may be contradictions or inconsistencies in the expectations attaching to a role. The headmaster may expect one way of behaving while a teacher's colleagues may expect quite another. For example, the headmaster may expect teachers to leave the staff room immediately on hearing the bell ringing to mark the end of the lunch hour. His reason for expecting this may be to ensure that teachers are in their classrooms when the children arrive. On the other hand, it may be an unwritten rule in the staff room that there should be no undue haste in reacting to the school bell. In this case a teacher who goes when the bell rings may be the subject of amusement or contempt on the part of his colleagues.

Role expectations, then, may be seen as a constraint on people's behaviour. They do not ensure that people will act in certain ways. They are pressures influencing people to act in ways approved by those who hold expectations of them. This is why it was said earlier that people act in *broadly* predictable ways. If a person occupies a certain position, and if we know anything about the role expectations which attach to that position, we can expect to sketch the outline of that person's behaviour. We cannot, however, predict what that person will do at any one time or in any given situation. There are a number of reasons for this. In the first place, as we have seen, role expectations are not all clear-cut and well understood. They may be unknown to the person until he has behaved in a certain way. Contradictory expectations may exist, held by different groups in contact with the person in question, and some expectations are firmer than others and exert more influence over the person. In the second place, everyone can be said to perform a number of roles. The teacher may be a husband, father, son, member of a local football team, a bridge club, and various professional committees. All of these positions will have role expectations attached to them, and they may well conflict with each other. A teacher's desire to put in extra time at school engaging in extra-curricular activities may be thwarted by his wife's insistence that for once he comes home early and plays with the children.

In the third place, there are other pressures on people which cannot easily be related to the roles they play. A person may want promotion and may therefore act in ways which he believes will gain him promotion. He may disregard, in so doing, other pressures and expectations coming from, for example, his peer group. Equally, he may have no hope of promotion at all and may therefore be impervious to some demands put on him which, if he wanted promotion, he would have to satisfy. Or a person may choose to act according to some system of values which he believes important rather than according to the demands of a role. For example, a teacher may be expected to punish physically children who are unruly in class. Physical punishment, however, may be abhorrent to him and he may refuse to employ it, even though the consequences of not doing so may include a noisy class and the contempt and disapproval of his colleagues and superiors.

In other words, role occupants are human beings who have a variety of influences working on them. As a result they do not act altogether in prescribed ways, even if there were always an agreed, prescribed way of behaving. They often act in ·unplanned ways and, partly by doing so, influence others to act in unplanned ways. There is a point of conflict here, of course, with those who are responsible for the management of the school. Managers such as headmasters and their senior colleagues have an interest in seeing that people act in planned ways in order that plans and policies can be carried out and procedures adhered to. They are responsible for ensuring that the school operates in an efficient way, that resources are used properly, and that children are educated. If they did not they might be brought to account by their employers, and also by irate parents and rate-payers. Much naturally depends on what is considered 'efficient', 'properly used' and 'educated'. Headmasters interpret this requirement in different ways, and depending on their interpretations, set orders of priorities, formulate policies and set up procedures. These inevitably affect the ways in which staff members do their jobs and the priorities and policies they themselves set.

Another influence on behaviour in the school is what may be called the 'culture' of the school. This culture, which consists of shared attitudes, beliefs, opinions and loyalties, derives from the organization's traditions, history, policies and procedures. The influence of the culture may be evident in statements such as 'this is the way we do things', 'that would never be done at our school', or 'we don't do things that way'. Implicit in these statements is an identification of the person *with* what is being done or the way it is being done. There is a process of learning what the 'correct' or accepted attitudes and responses are to particular situations. Loyalty often follows either because people genuinely believe that their school's policies and procedures are the best or, at least, good ways of doing things, or else because they do not like to be identified with policies and procedures about which they are uneasy. There are also pressures to conform and be loyal and it is not an easy matter for a teacher to be continuously critical where his friends and colleagues are satisfied with their situation.

People do retain their individuality, and loyalty is not always blind and undiscriminating. They may agree with some things and disagree with others, judging according to the pressures on them and the values they hold important. Perhaps even more important than attachment to an organization, and loyalty to the shared culture of that organization, are attachments and loyalties to the groups within the organization to which a person belongs —important in the sense of having consequences for that person's actions. A teacher may be highly critical of the school in which he works and may dislike the headmaster and his policies, but he may nevertheless be heavily influenced by the group or groups to which he belongs. These groups may contain his friends and closest colleagues, the people by whom he judges his own actions and performance. He may, therefore, identify much more closely with them than with the school.

Within the school there are three broad groups of people. There are teachers, including the headmaster although he may not teach, pupils and auxiliary staff such as janitors, catering staff, secretaries and others. These groups of people have different kinds of involvement in the school. The auxiliary staff are often kept separate from all issues other than those which concern them directly in their work. Teaching staff, in contrast, are expected to take a 'professional interest' in the pupils and in the life of the school, which exceeds the demands of their contracts. They may also be included in some of the decisions made in the school.

Teaching staff are seen as members of the school. They have a contract with the local authority which specifies the school but may also refer to the possibility of transfer to another school. They have a salary, and terms and conditions of appointment. They may belong to a professional organization which negotiates salaries and conditions of employment and which may intervene on their behalf with the local authority (as in the case of the Teesside dispute which we have already discussed). They hold meetings, working parties and conferences to decide on common approaches to the government and local authorities, and to discuss matters relating to pupils. They may be promoted out of the schools to the Inspectorate or to the education authority's administrative staff. Pupils, of course, are also seen as members of the school, but, as they are in general compulsorily recruited to schools, it is clear that we are dealing with two different kinds of membership. This is not simply a difference in rank, it is a difference in kind.

Teaching staff participation in decisions varies greatly from school to school. In some schools the head may hold regular meetings with his staff although he may stress that these are for the purpose of giving information and that they are not decision-making meetings. In other schools staff meetings may be held only very occasionally. Some headmasters work through smaller committees of staff, and others prefer to work mainly with individual members of staff. Whatever the case it is a safe assumption that there are times when the head must seek the co-operation of his staff. This is not true in the case of pupils, although the headmaster may seek their co-operation from personal inclination or from a belief that that is the best way of attaining his objectives. There may be arrangements whereby some pupils are appointed to junior 'administrative' positions, as in the case of prefects, form captains and class leaders, but the headmaster does not have to seek their co-operation and does not have to consult them. Many heads do not in fact do so.

Teaching staff, in general, have a choice of school and apply for particular jobs in particular schools. Apart from the possibility of private schooling, which does not exist for the majority of pupils, pupils have no choice of school, as they are allocated to schools on the basis of zoning arrangements drawn up by the local authority. It is usually extremely difficult to go outside these arrangements except to private schools. Teaching staff and pupils are both affected by administrative decisions taken in schools, but the staff are in a different position in that they have recourse to their professional organizations, which can lobby for or against proposed changes, and fight against alleged injustices. They can also resign and move to another school or local authority. To say this is not to minimize the difficulties involved in such actions. Nevertheless the possibilities exist. They do not exist for the pupils or for their parents, although we should note that efforts have been made to form a pupils' union and that parents' pressure groups are becoming more numerous.

Among the teaching staff themselves, there are many groups. There are, for example, promoted and unpromoted staff, departmental groups, and friendship groups. Departmental groups may have friendship links. Members of departments may have tea or coffee together, and spend part of their free time together. This would not be surprising, as they have interests and problems in common. Whether the head of department is included in such activities will depend on how relaxed are the relationships between him and his staff. Heads of departments themselves form another identifiable group. They also have interests and problems in common. The headmaster and his senior staff, such as the deputy head, senior mistress, assistant heads, and heads of school form another grouping. Across this pattern are imposed other groupings of people who are friendly and like to spend their time together, of of people who, for one reason or another, have to work together perhaps for only a limited time. Groups may be relatively isolated from each other. Departments whose classrooms are situated far from the main body may be thrown into their own company more than usual. The staff room may be a long way away and they may, therefore, decide to make their own tea or coffee rather than waste time. The house staff also, may spend most of their free time in their offices interviewing or simply being available to pupils. As a result they may only rarely visit the staff room and will, therefore, have few occasions for meeting the rest of the staff and talking with them, exchanging views, and explaining what they are doing. This may be particularly so if the house accommodation has been purpose built and is separated from the rest of the school. Finally, another group who may be isolated in the same way includes the headmaster and his senior staff. In some schools this group meets during breaks and lunch hours, thus ensuring that the degree of interaction with the rest of the staff is limited. Some headmasters avoid going to the staff room on the grounds that the staff ought to have somewhere to go away from the eyes and ears of the headmaster. Other heads see the staff room as a useful place for meeting the staff informally, and perhaps also as a place for transacting some business of a fairly unimportant kind, or of a kind which they think is best done in an informal atmosphere.

At the beginning of this chapter it was said that behaviour is constrained by structure in an attempt to produce activities which will lead to the achievement of desired goals. School organization, however, is complex and naturally imperfect and the structures which are set up do not always function in intended ways. Nor do activities necessarily lead to desired goals. In fact, the goals which are pursued in schools by the various individuals and groups may not always be compatible. There are clearly possibilities for conflict here. Conflict of goals, for example, may often occur between pupils and staff. Pupils have their own interests and will not always be willing to co-operate with the staff in attempting to achieve the goals the staff set for them. They may be opposed to the school and what the staff are trying to do, and if this is so, or even simply if the staff believe it to be so, the chief objective of the staff may change from one of teaching to one of control. There are also possibilities of conflict inherent in the teaching situation. Classes are often stable groups, whose members are able to develop relationships over a prolonged period. Teachers, on the other hand, meet these classes at intervals only for relatively short periods of time.

Conflict may also occur between departments, although most of the members of each department may not be parties to the conflict, which may engage primarily the heads of the departments concerned and such powerful allies as they can muster. Such conflict may occur when subjects are timetabled together. A timetable may be constructed in such a way that pupils in the middle and senior school cannot take, for example, both science and art, or both modern languages and technical subjects. In cases such as these the most able pupils are often encouraged or directed away from art and technical subjects. These departments may, not unnaturally, be unhappy about such a situation.

The kind of choice which a school can offer to its pupils is affected by the number of pupils in the school and the availability of staff. Academic criteria will also play a part in the allocation of resources. The headmaster and his staff will want to provide their pupils with the best education possible within the constraints acting upon them. Nevertheless, the allocation of a school's resources inherent in decisions bearing upon the structure of the curriculum and the construction of the timetable may also reflect decisions other than those which flow from these constraints. The fact that schools with broadly similar staffing problems and pupil numbers differ in their allocation of time and resources to the various subject areas indicates that there are other than academic criteria at work. Or else, that academic criteria vary considerably. Probably both indications are relevant. Academic criteria do differ considerably.

The beliefs and goals of the headmaster and his staff would also be important criteria, as would the moral assumptions they make about how resources should be allocated. We would also have to include, however, the results of the interplay between the headmaster and the heads of departments prior to the construction of the curriculum and the timetable. In other words we would have to take account of political activity in the school. In the examples we referred to above, the heads of the art and technical departments may couch their objections in terms which gave the impression that they were concerned only about the type of education the pupils were receiving. The headmaster and the other heads of departments, particularly those most likely to be affected in the event of any changes, may in turn interpret these objections in terms of the concern of the heads of the art and technical departments at the numbers and quality of the pupils they had to teach. In other words such a situation may be perceived by the participants as having political aspects. This may mean that the headmaster and those of his staff who object to the proposed changes need not pay serious attention, from an academic point of view, to the suggestions made.

Individuals may experience conflict because of competing or contradictory expectations about their behaviour. Presumably each role in the school will have its own attendant constellation of difficulties and conflicts as it is made up of expectations held by different individuals and groups, each with different interests and objectives. The headmaster, for example, has to reconcile, as best he can, conflicting expectations held by different groups and persons in the school, as well as those held by the education authority, parents and other outside groups. The teacher has to cope with the demands of his pupils and the demands of his colleagues and superiors. The deputy headmaster has possibly the most difficult job of all, as he has to be on good terms with the headmaster and keep the confidence of the staff. To examine some of the difficulties which may be built into an individual's situation, we shall look in more detail at the role of the assistant headmaster in a Scottish school.

Depending on the size of the school, there may be up to five assistant headmasters. These positions are relatively new and are developing in a variety of ways, depending on a number of factors, such as the objectives of the local education authority, the objectives of the headmaster of each school, the opportunities he allows for development, and the personalities and capabilities of the holders of the posts themselves. In some authorities there may be a horizontal division of the school into upper, middle and lower schools, with an assistant headmaster in charge of each. Alternatively, there may be an assistant head in charge of matters relating to the curriculum, one in charge of the system of guidance in the school, and another in charge of leisure activities.

There are certain general aspects of the job, however, which are likely to pertain whatever the division of responsibilities. In the first place, the job involves two different major activities: teaching, and, what we will call for the sake of brevity, administration (in other words, all those activities apart from teaching which he is required to do and for which he is paid his salary as an assistant headmaster). Teaching, of course, is timetabled, but his other activities are not and he cannot, therefore, predict with certainty when administrative activity will be required. It is quite likely that his teaching will be interrupted by the administrative demands of his job. If the interruptions are frequent they may frustrate the sustained attention which good teaching usually demands. Similarly, there will be occurrences in the school which he would like to be able to deal with immediately but cannot, because he is timetabled to teach.

Secondly, and related to this, his administrative commitments may bring him into conflict with the principal teacher of his department. The fact that the assistant headmaster may often be late for his classes or called away from them frequently, may disturb his head of department whose main concern and responsibility will be the teaching of the department. The third aspect also concerns the fact that assistant heads are teachers in a department. In some cases the assistant head, who will probably have been a principal teacher prior to his promotion, may be more experienced than his head of department. If he has been promoted within the school, he will find himself acting as a teacher in the department under a new principal teacher (who may have been one of his assistants before they were both promoted). In one school a new principal teacher had, as 'assistants' in her department, the deputy headmaster and an assistant headmaster, both of whom had been heads of that department prior to their promotions. In cases such as this, the assistant head may resist innovations made by the new principal, and even if he does not the latter may feel unsure about issuing directives to one who is only nominally his subordinate.

Fourthly, most other members of staff spend most of their time teaching and this makes it difficult for the assistant headmaster to contact them. Consequently, especially if all members of staff are not directly accessible by phone, a great deal of movement about the school is often necessary. Fifthly, there is the professional commitment to teaching. Assistant headmasters often say that they like teaching and would not want a job which did not allow them to teach. When they are promoted to headships, of course, their opportunities for teaching, particularly in a large school, will be limited. It is likely that this attitude is stimulated not only by their own past experience and by their no doubt genuine professional commitment, but also by the suspicion on the part of their colleagues, and in particular the principal teachers, about the proliferation of positions not exclusively concerned with teaching.

The role of the assistant headmaster is clearly an ambiguous one. He retains substantial teaching commitments, spending at least half of his time teaching, yet he is an important figure in the administration of the school. Indeed, his teaching commitments may often take second place to pressing organizational or administrative demands. On the one hand, there is the difficulty faced by the person who is professionally trained to teach, being appointed to an essentially bureaucratic job and, on the other hand, there is the possible antagonism of the other senior professional people in the organization who stress the professional requirements of the job and ignore or undervalue the other requirements. The role also has ambiguous implications for the pre-existing structure of the school. In the first place, as we have noted, the assistant head is subordinate in the teaching aspects of his job to the head of his department and this situation may pose problems for both the assistant head and for the head of department. In the second place, the assistant heads are subordinate to the headmaster and the deputy headmaster, and superior to heads of departments, but they are not necessarily in direct superior-subordinate relationship with the latter. They are perhaps assistants to the headmaster rather than assistant headmasters. They would appear to be in a co-ordinating rather than a directing role. The position may be somewhat different for an assistant head who is charged with control of the guidance system, where the superior-subordinate relationship may be clearer. In addition, of course, the guidance staff are fairly recent appointments themselves and have not had the time to build up the same sort of tradition of independence and prestige as is the case with the heads of departments. Because the situation is a new one, little or no consensus has yet been established about the role of the assistant headmaster, nor is there an established pattern of activities. Much still depends on what the headmaster wishes them to do and also what they manage to take on themselves. This situation naturally creates difficulties for the assistant headmasters, but it also has consequences for other people in the school. The principal teachers, for instance, are unclear about the ways in which the new appointments will affect them. They may fear that the creation of these positions will lessen the availability of the head-master to them, and that the insertion of a new rank between them and the head will mean a loss of status.

In this chapter a number of influences on people's behaviour in schools have been discussed. These included their goals, role expectations, the different groups to which people belong, and what has been called the 'culture' of the school. We have also seen that conflict may develop because the goals which some people pursue are incompatible with those pursued by others; because of the way activity in the school is structured and because of the factors influential as to the kind of structure adopted (such as goals, beliefs, moral assumptions, and political activity); and because of contradictory or unclear role expectations. It is important to note that all of these influences on behaviour are themselves inter-related and that the behaviour which occurs will itself influence and change the factors influencing it, for example, the goals which people are attempting to achieve will affect role expectations. This may be most evident as goals change, or as new goals are formulated. If the classics department in a school, which was formerly engaged in teaching classics to 'academic' pupils, becomes involved with other departments in teaching 'European studies' to less able pupils,

F

a different kind of behaviour will clearly be expected of the members of the department.

The same general point should be made about the structure of this book so far. For the sake of convenience and in an attempt at clarification, the school has been discussed under a number of headings: the environment, the goals of the school, its structure, and the influences on the behaviour of people within the school. In reality it is very difficult to isolate these. The environment affects the goals of a school in a number of ways. What people are trying to do in schools will reflect in part what is considered right and proper for schools to try to do. Some goals are set for the school, an example being the statutory requirement to provide religious education. Another example occurs when a local authority decides that its schools should put more effort into the social development of their pupils and may emphasise this by appointing staff to the school specifically for that purpose. Radical change in the goals of a school may be attempted where a local authority decides to change the school from being a grammar school to being a comprehensive school.

The relationships work the other way too. What schools are attempting to achieve, and perhaps more importantly, the changes which they make in the type and scope of their objectives, will alter people's ideas about what is right and proper for schools to do. Schools which adopt sex education programmes will, by their example, be influential in helping people to decide whether they think it right and proper for schools to involve themselves in such an activity. The fact that in many schools religious education is considered a burden to be carried and a requirement to be met at a minimal level, may eventually contribute to a climate of opinion which makes it possible for this requirement to be repealed. Although, here again the fact that religious education is in decline is partly a result of the decline of religion in the wider society. The example of some schools in laying more stress on the social development of their pupils than on their academic attainment, has been instrumental in persuading local authorities to support such a development in other schools. The goals pursued in a school will also influence its relationships with its local environment. An obvious example of this occurs where a school adopts the goal of involvement with the community and sends its pupils into the community in ways such as those we have discussed earlier.

The environment also influences behaviour in schools. Pupils' behaviour depends partly on their home backgrounds and the areas in which they live. Staff behaviour is influenced by current ideas as to the correct behaviour of teachers. Looking at it the other way, the activities of teachers in schools will influence what is accepted as correct behaviour. Experiments made by teachers in teaching methods and the content of teaching help to change the training they are given. The difficulties they have in meeting the requirements of outside bodies will affect the expectations held by those bodies, such as examining boards and local authorities. And pupil behaviour in schools, to the extent to which their behaviour is modified during their stay at school, will have consequences for their home life.

The environment determines in part the structure of the school. Ideas about the academic and social organization of pupils, for example house or tutor groupings, streaming and mixed-ability groupings, will come to schools from other schools, inspectors, and other outside sources. Equally, experiments made on these and similar lines by individual schools will have an effect on their environment in the shape of current educational ideas. The way in which the school is structured will also affect the school's everyday dealings with its environment. If the job of liaison with the school's feeder primary schools is allocated to some specific person, such as an assistant headmaster, we might expect to see a difference in the relationship between the school and its feeder primary schools, than if there were no formal allocation of the job, or if the headmaster fitted it in as best he could.

The behaviour of the members of a school, the activities in which they are involved and the conflicts which occur, will influence the structure of the school. Role definitions and expectations, for example, may be modified as a result of conflict caused by existing structural arrangements. An example of this might be where the deputy headmaster of a school has for a long time concerned himself with careers advice to pupils. A careers master may be appointed in order to improve the quality and extend the range of careers advice in the school. Conflict may arise between the deputy headmaster and the careers master because their working relationship has not been adequately defined. As a result of this it may be decided to define their relationship more exactly, or to remove the deputy head from the area of careers advice, or to abolish the post of careers master. In each case, structural alterations may be said to have been made as a consequence of the conflict.

The whole pattern of relationships in the school, the formal structure as well as the informal relationships between people, will affect the way they behave, in terms of the activities required of them and their assessments of correct behaviour. From the other point of view, what people actually do, the perhaps slight differences between what they do and what is formally required of them, will have consequences for the structure of the school.

CHAPTER 5

Management in Schools

In comparison with developments in the industrial and commercial sectors, management principles have come relatively recently to schools and other educational organizations. Management has been thought of as something that occurred in commercial firms. It was concerned with profits, sales and strikes and other such things, which were no concern of those who were responsible for schools. Apart from the fact that people considered such a statement to be factually true, there was an element of disdain involved. Education was rigidly separated from the world of work. From another point of view this was and remains one of the most powerful indictments of what goes on in schools. It is precisely the irrelevance of what they were taught in schools to what they did afterwards, which has been the substance of the complaint of so many adults, all of them former school pupils. Of course, there is a whole argument here about what is or should be involved in education, about the difference between education and training, about the importance of having some degree of insight into historical, cultural and scientific knowledge.

In any event, isolation from the world of work did help to foster the attitude that management was an activity which had no relevance to schools, colleges and universities, and that, consequently, management thought was not something with which teachers and headmasters needed to concern themselves. Another factor in the situation was that management research, in the early stages at least, was concerned primarily with industrial organizations. The urge to increase profits was in fact, one of the main motives behind so much of this research. Furthermore, there were people, other than school teachers, who thought that management was a function of business enterprises only. Peter Drucker, a well-known writer on management, says that "The first definition of management is . . . that it is an economic organ". This means that "The skills, the competence, the experience of management cannot, as such, be transferred and applied to the organization and running of other institutions". A career in management was not, by itself, a preparation for political office, or for leadership in the Armed Forces, the Church or a university.

> "The skills, the competence and the experience that are common and therefore transferable are analytical and administrative—extremely important, but secondary to the attainment of the primary objectives of the various non-business institutions. Whether Franklin D. Roosevelt was a great President or a national disaster has been argued hotly in this country for twenty years. But the patent fact that he was an extremely poor administrator seldom enters the discussion; even his staunchest enemies would consider it irrelevant. What is at issue are his basic political decisions".[11]

One can take issue with Drucker here without denying that the primary function of management in a business firm is an economic one, and without wishing to imply that someone who has been successful in managing a business will, therefore, be successful in running a school or a university. It is, as Drucker implies, a question of knowledge and skill. Basic educational decisions distinguish schools from one another. This in no way implies that analytical and administrative skills are unimportant in schools. In fact quite the opposite. Analytical and administrative skills may make all the difference between succeeding in putting into effect basic educational decisions and failing to do so. Whichever view we take there can be no argument about the fact that it is now recognized that schools are 'managed' and that many people now believe that something can be done to ensure that they are better managed. There have been several factors at work in preparing the way for this change. In the first place, research interests have broadened to include organizations other than commercial firms. A substantial amount of social science research has been done into schools, hospitals, and other non-commercial organizations. An increasing proportion of this research has an organizational perspective.

Secondly, there have been changes in the vocabulary used to describe political activity. We hear talk about the way the government is managing the economy, and about business managers managing the affairs of political parties. In the 1960s Edward Heath and Harold Wilson came to be seen as political leaders forged in the image of managers more explicitly than any of their predecessors. In these circumstances, traditional political judgements seemed to be displaced by a premium put on administrative competence (or the lack of it) which we were discussing earlier. Perhaps things have changed since Roosevelt's day.

Thirdly, there have been a number of developments inside industry. One of these was a recognition that managers could be trained. Heavy reliance might still be placed on native wit and ability but it was thought that there were some aspects of management which a manager could master by learning from the experience of others. There are certain technical aspects such as production control, marketing and accounting which can be taught as well as areas such as problem-solving and decision-making. At the same time there was an increase in the use of management consultants in an effort to solve the problems of individual firms. Other developments were the establishment of business schools at Manchester and London, and the growth at other universities and colleges of interests in the area of management training.

Management training has also been accepted in the Civil Service since the Fulton Report of 1968, which recommended that a Civil Service College should provide training courses in administration and management. Hospital and local government administrators are also beginning to look at ways in which management training could be relevant to them. Finally, in the area of education, interest begins to blossom in management training. The British Educational Administration Society which was formed in 1971, is an indication of the growing interest in management education. Universities, polytechnics and colleges are becoming increasingly involved in framing courses for educational administrators.

Although one can greet this new-found interest in management education among educationists with approval, it is also important to point out that there are dangers in this situation. In the first place, it can be easily assumed that management education covers an agreed body of knowledge which the practitioners in these new business schools, university departments or training college management units can distil at will to their students. This is not the case. In the second place, the content of management education courses can range widely, including, for example, budget control, sensitivity training, critical path analysis and public relations. One senior British executive said recently that you can learn all you need about management education inside six weeks, the rest of the time you should be studying politics. Political skill, in his eyes, was the cornerstone of such education. Moreover, the methods of teaching management education are themselves much more varied than one would normally find in university departments or teacher training colleges. Simulation exercises, role-playing, case studies, sensing meetings, model-building, are only some of the methods used in management education. In other words, it is important for students of school organization to be aware that management education may well mean different things to different people. It may mean one-day pep talks for industrial supervisors, or a three-year sandwich course, or a four-year full-time degree course in administration.

It might be useful to attempt some categorization of what is, at first glance, a bewildering picture of intellectual subjects and teaching methods. We can profitably regroup these various activities into three main categories. In the first place, what is frequently meant by management education is the acquisition of skills and competences that will assist the manager in achieving certain ends. Budget control, statistical sampling, and discounted cash flow, would be examples of management techniques which managers can learn to help them solve their problems. This is, by far, the easiest aspect of management education to comprehend, and, or course, by far, the easiest to teach. Managers can usually recognize the necessity for better work methods, improved financial controls or better marketing techniques. Similarly, attempts have been made in the past to find computerized solutions to timetabling problems, and studies have been made of the work of school clerical staff. The new interest in management education is in part a realization that there are a great many techniques available within management which different kinds of managers can utilize.

Secondly, it is obvious that the acquisition of such skills as work study would not by itself have been a convincing argument to have secured the support of universities and other august bodies. Some other arguments would have had to be used, principally that management education provided the student with a broad conceptual approach to the whole managerial process. The debate that went on in the early 1960s about introducing management education into universities hinged on this concept, in other words, that management education could not be introduced unless it was based on respectable academic disciplines. The supporters of such an introduction argued from the fact that engineering and medicine were mainly vocational, but still firmly established within universities. Basic studies or framework subjects, as they were sometimes called, would leaven the teaching of managerial techniques. Mathematics, economics, psychology, statistics could be among the contenders for such studies and, along with basic research into the facts of organizations, would allow the establishment of management education in our higher education institutions. Evidence of this broader conceptual approach in the area of educational administration can be found in textbooks which deal with concepts of authority and power and aspects of organizational theory.

Thirdly, what one often finds as management education is a concern with human behaviour in organizations. It is this aspect which usually encourages the view that management cannot be taught at all. The argument concedes that there is some use in providing a broad background of knowledge in law or economics for a manager, or in training him in some technique like work study, but denies the possibility of improving his behaviour. In other words one could illustrate the importance of workers' attitudes or group behaviour, but there could be no guarantee that this would change the manager's behaviour. This position has been so heavily attacked over the last twenty years that in many places it has been replaced by a definition of management which sees it as a process by which the manager organizes other people's behaviour in relation to the physical means and resources in order to achieve desired goals—in other words, by a definition of management which sees it in behavioural terms. Given such a perspective, it would follow that the ways in which managers managed to get people to work effectively would become important and, in a sense, the history of management education can be reviewed as the history of how complex this problem of managing to get people to work effectively actually is. Management education, in other words, became associated with the behavioural subjects of status systems, motivation, perception, communications and decision-making.

In the early days, at the turn of the century, the overall concern was with increasing worker efficiency and, thereby, the output and profit of the firm. Frederick Taylor[12], who is usually credited with pioneering the engineering or scientific approach to management, encouraged detailed studies of methods of work and the discovery of the 'one best way' of doing particular jobs. 'Best' was determined in terms of the speed with which a task could be performed and the fatigue which resulted. The 'one best way', was, therefore, the way which involved the maximum speed with the minimum of fatigue. Payment was tied as closely as possible to output on the assumption that workers were motivated primarily by the economic rewards and would, therefore, work harder if they could see clearly the financial rewards. Such a simplistic view of human beings has held sway for a long time. One might point out that a great deal of our industrial relations are bedevilled by such a crude assumption about human beings. By the end of the 1920s, however, this view of management as work engineering was challenged. Vying for consideration were such factors as work norms, groups to which the workers belonged, workers' feelings and attitudes, non-economic rewards and sanctions, different leadership patterns and methods of communication. All of these were now being presented as important elements in the work situation and hence in the education of managers. As the behavioural sciences developed, these factors almost became academic subjects in their own right; certainly, experts in these subjects appeared on the scene in Europe and North America.

A great deal of this work has been displaced in the late 1950s and in the 1960s by a number of fuller perspectives of human beings. The American psychologist, Maslow[13], posited a hierarchy of needs to which all of us are subject. In the first place, he said, physiological needs such as hunger, thirst and sex have to be satisfied. Then comes the need for safety from danger. Third are the needs for warm relationships with others. Fourth are the needs for respect from others and self-respect. Last are the needs for self-actualization or self-fulfilment, the need to fulfil one's own potential and to express oneself. This theory underpinned a number of management theories, some of which gained great prominence in the United States and in this country, and became almost overnight part of the folk-lore of management. Douglas McGregor, for example, in his book *The Human Side of Enterprise* (1960)[14] articulated two alternative theories of management which he called Theory X and Theory Y. His purpose was to examine the assumptions on which managerial strategies rested. Theory X assumed that people had to be directed, motivated, controlled, rewarded and punished in order to produce behaviour consistent with the needs of the organization. Management's job was to do the directing and controlling, the motivating, rewarding and punishing. The assumption was that without a panoply of controls and motivations people would work as little as possible and ignore the needs of the organization for which they worked. Theory Y, on the other hand, assumed much more of a concordance between individual and organizational interests. People were not naturally lazy and given the opportunity and the right conditions would accept responsibility and behave in a way consistent with the needs of the organization. The job of management was to produce these 'right conditions and to bring about a realization of the concordance between individual and organizational interests'.

A third writer, Frederick Herzberg[15], argued that there were two sets of factors important to people's motivation at work. One set of factors, called hygiene factors, included company policy and administration, supervision, salary, inter-personal relations and working conditions. These factors appeared to be related to job dissatisfaction.

The second set of factors, called motivators, included achievement, recognition, work itself, responsibility and advancement. These factors appeared to lead to job satisfaction. Each set of factors seemed to work only the one way. In other words, factors leading to job satisfaction did not seem particularly relevant in cases of job dissatisfaction. The implications of this theory were that administrative procedures, salaries and working conditions are minimum conditions to be satisfied. If they are not adequate people will be dissatisfied. In order to promote positive satisfaction, however, other factors have to be attended to, relating to job content and doing the job to the satisfaction of one's superiors.

The notion of self-actualization was an influential one. Certainly, if you ask senior managers in the fields of education, health, police and industry what were the circumstances in which they felt that they worked effectively, the answer is usually along the lines that they were recognized and praised by their bosses, or had experienced feelings of importance or had met some exceptional challenge or had been left alone to get on with their work or had had a sense of achievement—in other words, the language of Maslow's top layer of hierarchical needs. Bradley and Wilkie in *The Concept of Organization* (1974)[16] have pointed out, however, that this new idea of self-actualization is really an old moral philosophical idea of self-realization brushed up in social psychological jargon. They go on to indicate some of the difficulties that the notion presents. Do we try to actualize all our potentialities? If not, which ones do we select for actualizing? How do we ensure our actualizing some potentiality is not frustrating your actualizing your potentiality? The notion seems to raise many more questions than it solves, but it has, at least, the merit of taking us out of the Dark Ages of management thought and bringing us up to the beginning of an Elizabethan era where human beings are now regarded as being slightly more complex than laboratory-trained rats. We have, of course, a long way to go before management theory comes of age and presents systematic discussion of human beings as human beings.

There have been, then, three broad aspects of management education: the training of the manager in managerial techniques, the broadening of the manager with basic or core subjects, and the development of his self-awareness and his awareness of his role. It is important to point out, however, that the conventional wisdom of these different aspects is being overshadowed by new developments in organizational analysis, of which this book, and the series of which it is a member, plays a small part. During the 1960s a completely new perspective on organizations emerged which views the organization as paramount. This has resulted from an awareness that management is much more complex than the previous theories would allow. In the early days of Taylor, management, as we saw, was viewed as dominated by the simple concerns of demonstrating the 'one best way' of achieving objectives. This was challenged in the 1930s '40s and '50s by strong recommendations for managers to concern themselves with the feelings and values of their subordinates. Personnel management blossomed and major organizations established sports clubs, canteens, playing fields, piped music and notice-boards. The various explorations of the idea of self actualization again shifted or extended the definition of management. The manager's task was to create the conditions in which his subordinates could actualize themselves. Only in the '60s, however, was the manager's task seen as related to the goals and structure of the organization, as well as its technology and the environment in which it operated. The manager's task was now being increasingly viewed as integrating and co-ordinating organizational resources—for example men, material, money—towards the accomplishment of objectives as effectively and efficiently as possible.

The organizational perspective, then, has thrown up a radically new way of viewing the whole management process. The growth of the subject in the last decade has created new sets of questions—about goals, technology, structure, compliance, organizational roles and motivation, information-decision-systems in organizations, and innovation. Managers nowadays must come to terms with these, and other issues. Such a new perspective made it much more possible to account for the success or failure of various methods of effecting change and improving performance within organizations. The dominance of 'one best way' led to the application of the various managerial techniques in all kinds of organizations. Management-by-objectives, for example, which had appeared successful in some industrial firms, was used as the panacea technique suitable for organizations as disparate as various Civil Service departments and the police. The new approach allows us to understand why such techniques were successful in the one case and unsuccessful in the next.

The growing awareness then, amongst those associated with education, that running a school has something to do with management is welcome, but we would also want to encourage a reorientation of such thinking towards a careful discriminating understanding of the school as an organization. Only from this perspective could educational administration benefit from the development of management theories and techniques in other fields. Without such a perspective, it would be more likely that a naïve but fashionable enthusiasm for management might lead to all sorts of harmful attempts to graft inappropriate ideas into the running of a school. This has happened in other contexts. Some of the most fundamental ideological tenets of the Roman Catholic church were totally disregarded in the report of a management consultancy firm brought in to improve the Church's administration. Not so long ago, a considerable *furor* arose over the discovery of a management report on the organization of Warwick

University which seemed to reject the principle of demo-
cratic representation in academic decision-making. Both
these examples should indicate the dangers that exist if the
adoption of a managerial perspective on the school stands
on nothing stronger than a shallow flirtation with the fads
and fancies in the latest managerial textbooks.

If we look then at the question, what is involved in
the management of a school, the organizational perspective
allows us to acknowledge the role of managerial activity
in the running of the organization. In every organization
there are people who occupy positions that give them the
authority to make decisions which make a difference to
the state of the organization. This difference may be in the
goals the organization pursues, the way it is structured to
pursue them, the involvement of members in the organization, or the means by which the organization relates to
various factors in its environment. If we accept that
management is the authorized co-ordination and utilization of human and material resources, we can recognize
that in the school there are many positions which give
such authorization to their occupants. Certainly the headmaster or headmistress of a large school will have
almost exclusively managerial duties to perform in the
school. In addition the current trend towards large comprehensive schools creates a number of senior posts that
are defined not in terms of their teaching content but in
terms of their administrative duties. Deputy heads, senior
masters and mistresses, heads of departments and house
positions are all roles in the school that draw their
distinctive characteristics from the way in which they fit
into the administrative system.

At the bottom of this system, teachers carry out the
mainstream activity of the school in face-to-face relations
with pupils, but even here the teaching role may be usefully analysed in terms of its managerial nature. Not
only do most teachers have some administrative duties
to perform, their teaching activity itself also involves

demands in terms of the co-ordination and utilization of resources. What they teach and how they teach it are by no means the exclusive product of their professional training—indeed they may not have undergone exclusively educational training. The organization of the school will be a persistent, pervasive and irresistible cluster of factors influencing the nature and quality of what teachers achieve in the classrooms.

For the purpose of this chapter, however, which is to elucidate the nature of management in the school, rather than to give a definitive account of it, it will be convenient if we concentrate on the role of the headmaster. This position enables its occupant to determine the precise nature of the administrative system of the school as a whole, and, as in most organizations, what occurs at the top is usually the best clue as to what is happening elsewhere in the organization. (Wildcat strikes, it is sometimes remarked, are often the result of wildcat management). There are three reasons why we shall concentrate on the headmaster. One: it is cumbersome in an introductory text to mention all the other occupants of administrative roles each time. Two: each school will be slightly different in the extent to which these other people are in fact involved and in the particular responsibilities which they carry. Three: the headmaster is usually influential in deciding what other people will do. Local authorities may appoint people to do specific jobs in a school but the headmaster will be instrumental in deciding the degree of content of each job, and will affect the amount of influence each of these people has on the decisions made in the school. There will, of course, be other factors in the situation such as the personality and ability of the particular person, and the degree of influence he has in the school as a whole.

In examining the role of the headmaster, the organizational perspective might focus, first of all, on the management of the school's relationship with its environment.

G

Some headmasters are much more involved in external activities than others, but every headmaster has to have some minimal contact with people and groups outside the school. For instance, all public schools have routine relations with their local authorities, and with government departments and other bodies, in the form of requests for statistical information, arrangements for external examinations, requests for incidental expenses, reporting repairs needed, and receiving circulars. Headmasters may also be involved in public relations activity. The term 'public relations' may be unusual because it normally denotes an attempt at securing public support for some body or set of activities. Some headmasters devote very little effort to such activity and attach little importance to public support as such. However, most headmasters will, at some time, be involved in explaining the goals, policies and procedures of their schools to persons outside the school.

Each school's relationship with its environment will depend on two broad factors. First, the environment itself. There are obvious differences in the geographical location of the school which lead to variations in the background and attitudes of parents and children. There may be special features to the environment, such as a situation in a city centre, or situation close to a dominant industry. Or else there may be a particular drugs problem in a nearby town. The second factor consists of the attitudes, interests and abilities of the school's staff. This factor will determine the attempts they make to combat disadvantages in the environment or to make use of advantages. The relationship with the environment is clearly critical in terms of the setting of goals and the factors affecting their achievement.

An organizational perspective would focus on the goal-setting activities of the school. Headmasters do not necessarily approach this aspect of their job in such a conscious way, but the chances are high that they will be involved in these activities without necessarily being able to articulate them. Even on appointment they may not have the chance to think about this, for there may well be a host of day-to-day activities waiting for decisions, which have to be attended to immediately. Nevertheless, it is part of the headmaster's job and the policies and procedures and structural arrangements he advocates, together with the decisions he takes and the consequences these have for school activity, will reflect the goals which the headmaster wishes the school to pursue. For instance, if a headmaster wants to ensure that pupils have a knowledge of the history, culture and science of their society, or if he wants to ensure that the school has a good academic reputation, this decision will have consequences for the curriculum structure and timetable of the school, as well as for the activities of the staff and, perhaps, for the organization of the pupils in the school. If, on the other hand, he wants to increase the social awareness of his pupils by, for example, developing a specific social education programme, this will have different consequences for the school, in terms of the activities of the staff, and also, perhaps, the amount of time and effort which is put into creating and developing a teaching programme in social education.

An understanding of the complexity of organizational goals would also allow the headmaster to be aware of the possibility of contradictory or competing goals. For example, if he wants to increase the social awareness of his pupils, how can he ensure that another of his goals, such as ensuring that the school has a good academic reputation, will not suffer when certain resources are diverted from it? Moreover, other people in the school may have goals which compete with or contradict the headmaster's goals and such conflict may take on proportions that significantly affect the achievement of the headmaster's goal.

Once the goals have been set, policies have to be decided. If goals are generalized objectives to which action is directed or is supposed to be directed, policies are the courses of action which are adopted to achieve goals. Thus, in order to achieve the goal of increasing social awareness of pupils, the headmaster may adopt the policy of developing a social education programme. In order to achieve the goal of ensuring that the school has a good academic reputation, he may concentrate on improving the results of external examinations. But goals and policies clearly interact. Goals determine the policies adopted in the school, but so do the policies adopted help to change goals, or to show how the goals are contradictory or competing. Policies adopted as a result of one goal may help to modify another goal. For example, a policy of increased staff consultation adopted in an attempt to contain staff disaffection may result in changes being made in the balance between academic and non-academic activities in the school. Headmasters are usually asked to rule on policies which cover the whole range of topics, including the organization of pupils, the existence and type of staff committees, the existence and type of pupil or staff-pupil committees, the kinds of decisions which may be taken by his staff, and educational visits outside the school. The policies they decide on will depend on the overall objectives they have in mind.

An organizational perspective would also focus on the setting-up of structural arrangements in the school. As we have noted earlier, there is a wide area of discretion left to the headmaster regarding the structure of the school. For example, the basic academic and social organization of the pupils, and the extent to which he wishes to use a structure of committees to help him in the administration of the school. He may want a committee of heads of departments to discuss, for example, curricular development and the timing of internal examinations. A committee of staff involved in pastoral guidance may be desirable to co-ordinate their activities. Should there be a committee made up of representatives of heads of departments and guidance staff to discuss points of common interest? To what extent are junior staff and pupils to be involved in advisory or decision-making committees? Decisions on structural arrangements will, of course, reflect the goals which the headmaster believes are important.

Particular jobs have to be allocated to particular individuals. The deputy head may be given a vague remit by the local education authority when he is appointed. It may state that he is to deputize for the headmaster when the latter is absent, or that he should assist the headmaster in the performance of his duties. In effect it means that what the deputy head does depends very much on what the headmaster wishes him to do. The same applies to other senior staff in the school. Even where broad areas are specified, in practice the range of responsibilities and activities engaged in depends to a large degree on the headmaster. Individual teachers may be asked to take responsibility for a variety of tasks, such as dealing with truancy, careers information and the setting up of a programme of careers talks, references for pupils who apply to universities, colleges or firms, and arranging courses for pupils in each year group.

Headmasters often receive requests to attend conferences, meetings and social occasions. They may not be able to attend themselves but feel that the school should be represented, in which case they may appoint a member of staff to go in their place. Some relations with the environment require more permanent arrangements. Liaison with primary schools is a good example, especially in the case of a large school which has a number of feeder schools. The arrangements will depend in part on the importance attached by the headmaster to this sort of relationship. Some schools appoint a senior member of staff to take special responsibility for visiting primary schools, talking to staff members and the new year's intake, and arranging visits to the secondary school.

Procedures also have to be decided on for a wide

range of activities in the school. There will be procedures for dealing with discipline problems; procedures for keeping track of individual pupils; procedures regarding the expenditure of money; procedures regarding the use of clerical staff; a whole host of procedures governing pupil movement and behaviour; procedures for interviewing pupils at specific times of the year; and procedures for reporting on their performance.

The fourth aspect on which an organizational perspective would focus is on the management of behaviour. Apart from setting goals, formulating policies, setting up procedures and structures, appointing people to jobs, headmasters also attempt to ensure that their policies are being carried out, that procedures are being adhered to, that people are doing their jobs properly, and that the activities of the school seem to be working towards the achievement of the goals. Similarly, they attempt to find out why policies are not being carried out (it may be that they are bad ones), why procedures are not being adhered to (perhaps they are unworkable) and why the goals of the school are not being attained (perhaps because they are unattainable or because people do not consider them worth attainment). In other words, they attempt to control behaviour.

Two activities are related to control. The first of these is co-ordination. If a number of activities are all related to one particular objective, it may be necessary to see that these activities are co-ordinated, although this will not necessarily be done by the headmaster. In one sense, of course, a large part of the headmaster's responsibility is concerned with co-ordination in that he has to co-ordinate the activities of the whole school to ensure among other things that the children receive a good education, however that may be defined. In the second place, activities have to be evaluated. Someone has to make a judgement as to whether the activities of the school or parts of it are likely to achieve the set objectives. Examinations are part of the evaluation process as they attempt to measure how successfully pupils have learned and how successfully teachers have taught. Other activities are not susceptible to this kind of evaluation, however, and other methods have to be found.

The other activity is communications. All managements have to communicate with their staffs, although the amount and kind of communication will vary depending in part on the attitude adopted by the managers. Headmasters have to communicate instructions, recommendations, requests and information to their staff. The extent to which these are received, understood and acted on will depend in part on the success of the communications system in the school. Because of the amount of communication necessary in a large school, some headmasters run (or appoint other people to run) internal news-sheets or diaries containing information about school activities, requests for pupils to attend interviews, notices of events affecting the staff and pupils, and instructions from the headmaster. Such news-sheets, however, will not be able to carry all communications. Some communications will be confidential or applicable to only a small number of staff and the news-letter may in any case be published only once or twice a week. A school may have a pigeon-hole system, but this has the defect that people may not clear their pigeon-holes often enough to receive last minute or short notice information. Other schools have Tannoy systems and provided that teaching is not continually interrupted by announcements, this may be an effective method. Another system is to send all urgent communications to heads of departments with an injunction to them to see that their department members receive the message. This method can only be used occasionally, however, and does not solve the basic problem. The system must also be able to cope with communications which have to be passed between other staff. That is, it has to be able to deal with horizontal as well as vertical communications. Whatever the answer chosen in individual schools, the problem is clearly a managerial one.

Another important aspect of a headmaster's job is managing the various kinds of conflict which occur in the school. There may be conflict over goals, policies and procedures; conflicts between members of staff, between teaching staff and clerical or janitorial staff, conflict between staff and pupils, or between pupils. Conflict can also occur with people or groups of people in the school's environment. Perhaps the most likely instances concern parents. Conflict with parents can occur because they do not appear to ensure that their children attend school regularly, or because they disagree with the courses which the school wishes their children to take, or because they dispute the academic assessment given to their children by the school. Conflict may also arise over disciplinary measures taken against a child, or over a teacher's supposed attitude to a child, or for any number of other reasons. Conflict can also occur with governors or local authorities over the activities of the school or the internal arrangements in the school. All of these different instances of conflict have, in some way, to be managed, whatever the particular response decided on. As we saw in chapter four, a number of such conflicts lies in the nature of the organization rather than in the personalities of the people manning it. An organizational perspective would help to differentiate them, and thus be directly relevant to the understanding of the management of a school.

Such an analysis should be an aid to clear thinking about the role of management in a school organization, rather than a means by which the behaviour of any particular headmaster may be described. This is because the categories provided by the organisational perspective are not empirically discrete and they overlap and interrelate in complex fashions. To any particular headmaster his job might appear as a seamless web of different activities, or his work might force him to deal with matters which fall into more than one of the categories mentioned above. An obvious example is the timetable. The decisions which result in the completed timetable will reflect the goals and policies of the school, as well as the academic organization of the pupils. The headmaster may allocate the actual process of drawing up the timetable (according to criteria which he has laid down) to one of his staff. There will be conflicts of interest between departments which will have to be resolved. Above all, perhaps, the time table is the embodiement of the headmaster's control over the activities of his school and the resources which are allocated to those activities. There will be other school activities which remain outside the control of the time table, although all are affected by it to some degree, but the bulk of a school's activities, together with the largest part of the time of both pupils and staff will be ordered by the time table.

We have argued for an organizational perspective of the managerial and administrative aspects of a school, and it has been suggested that such a perspective should underpin the more overtly managerial training and education which has become fashionable. And additional value of such an analysis, however, is that it allows one to identify much more easily the peculiar features of the organization —why it is that student behaviour under pressure differs from that of car workers, why one laboratory is better than another, why there is a high turnover of tellers in one bank rather than another. The school is an organization in its own right. It has particular features which bear upon the school manager's job and act as constraints on his decisions and actions.

In the first place, there is the basic teacher-class situation. Under normal circumstances the teacher is alone with his class and no direct supervision can be exercised over his work, although supervision can take the form of evaluation of his teaching in terms of class results, and evaluation of his control over his classes in terms of the level of noise which comes from his classrooms. The methods by which he produces these results and exercises control over his classes are much more difficult to supervise. Almost impossible to supervise are the ways in which he presents himself as an adult to the children, the moral conceptions which he communicates to them, and the attitudes, beliefs and prejudices which are implicit or explicit in his behaviour. Under these circumstances it is difficult to ascertain whether the behaviour of individuals is directed towards pursuing the goals of the school. The teacher-class situation also produces many of the conflicts which have to be settled by the headmaster and communications between members of staff are hindered by the fact that teachers are in class for most of the day.

In the second place, there is the difficulty of evaluating the school's activities. Measures of evaluation are hard to come by apart from the traditional one of evaluation by examination. Examinations are themselves crude and unsatisfactory measures except in cases where one of the goals of a school might be to improve examinations results. For other kinds of goals, they are inadequate. This means, among other things, that the headmaster will have difficulty in assessing whether in fact his school is turning out pupils who will be responsible adults and useful members of society or whether his pupils will be able to cope with a greater amount of leisure time, if these are among his goals. It is also, as we have noted, difficult to evaluate the work of individual teachers because of the circumstances in which they work.

The third feature concerns the disagreement which may exist between staff over the aims of the school. A distinction has been drawn earlier in this book between personally-oriented goals and organizationally-oriented goals. All staff in schools as in other organizations will have their own personal objectives, such as looking for promotion or avoiding it, and getting a better share of upper school teaching. Such aims may well affect the way in which they work for their organizationally-oriented goals. What is at issue here are differences among the staff as to what the school as a whole should be aiming for. These differences will affect the way in which they work for the set aims of the school. Schools are perhaps different from some other organizations in this respect. If you work for a company which produces nuts and bolts then you presumably have little scope for argument about what the company should be doing. You may have reservations as to the way the company produces the nuts and bolts or as to the wisdom of its marketing or personnel policies, but if you do not like producing nuts and bolts, you have theoretically at least, the option of moving elsewhere to work which is more congenial to you.

It is true that in teaching also, if you do not like what happens in your school you also have the option of moving elsewhere until you find a school with whose aims you are in agreement. However, the problem is a broader one than that, because there is no consensus, or at most a limited consensus, as to what 'education' means and what schools should be doing in order to educate children. Within most schools there is likely to be a range of opinion on these issues. Under such circumstances the process of goal-setting will clearly not be without difficulties. Since the structures and procedures of the school will be influenced by the goals which are set, there may also be difficulties in getting these to work satisfactorily. Conflicts may also be expected in such a situation, and there are obvious difficulties in control and evaluation.

A fourth feature of the school concerns the possible lack of internal control over appointments and dismissals. Schools differ again here from many other types of organizations. This is not to say that in many cases the headmaster is not influential in decisions about staffing appointments. In fact there seems to be a great deal of variation in the extent to which headmasters are involved. Appointments legally rest, however, with the local education authority. This circumstance is important because unless he is able to choose his staff, or, at least, exercise a veto on appointments, his freedom to choose people for particular responsibilities will be curtailed. Furthermore, goal-setting will take place in the context of a staffing situation over which he has limited control, and activities ostensibly leading to the achievement of the headmaster's goals will be performed by people who are not necessarily in sympathy with these goals.

A fifth feature of the school is that it is full of specialist staff. The headmaster is unlikely to know very much about the areas of competence of departments other than his own specialism. In these circumstances it is clearly difficult for him to exercise a substantial measure of control over the aims of the departments in their teaching. It is also difficult for him to know to what extent the departments are keeping up with new developments in their fields, and in general to evaluate the work of the departments. There is the related difficulty of adjudicating between the competing claims of departments for the resources of the school. Reliable criteria on which to base judgements may be hard to find.

A complicating factor is that teachers are professionals who may resist what they see as the encroachment of organizational authority into areas which they would regard as within their professional competence. In addition, the departmentalization of the school may breed local loyalties which compete with school loyalties. Departments may also become isolated particularly if their classrooms are apart from the school's main buildings. Courses run by more than one department where the departments have to co-operate closely together with experiments such as team teaching may counteract this tendency.

The school has to operate according to rules and procedures determined outside the school and this constitutes a sixth feature adding to the complexity of management. Government regulations have to be complied with and there is the whole range of rules and regulations emanating from the local authority. These influences provide a framework within which the school manager must operate. It is only after these requirements are satisfied that the school manager can begin to set up his own structures and procedures.

One of the most important features of the school, of course, is the presence of children. They are unlike the passive raw materials which, in other organizations, are processed in order to manufacture goods. They have values and interests which are different from those of the staff. There are other influences working on them outside the school, such as parents, friends, cinema, television and other media and churches. They may, accordingly, be resistant to the aims of the staff. Inside the school they have relations with other pupils who may be more influential than staff members. They are, in fact, human. They are not in the same position as human beings in other institutions by virtue of their age. They do not have the same rights as staff members of schools, for example. They have no powerful trade unions or professional organizations to look after their interests. They cannot go on strike without fear of victimization. They are subject to physical punishment at the discretion of their teachers.

We are now in a better position to ask the question— is it useful to think of the headmaster as a manager? Will it make any difference to the way schools are run? There are three possible results which we might expect from a recognition of management activity. In the first place, we might expect that it would contribute to the better management of schools for school managers to be aware that what they are doing is managing. This is not to say that one would want headmasters to start thinking and acting according to some image they might have of the ways in which a manager should think or act. What is necessary is a recognition that what happens in schools is not simply 'education', and that headmasters are not simply teachers.

In the second place, we could expect consequences for the training of headmasters. By recognizing certain activities as management activities we are opening the way for a recognition that management skills are involved, and that these skills may be different from those that are necessary for teaching. Management skills are critical where goals and policies have to be decided on, structures set up and control exercised. The particular kinds of goals and policies, the particular kinds of structure set up, and the kinds of control exercised will demand educational decisions and, therefore, educational knowledge and experience. But the setting of the goals and the securing of agreement for them, the setting up of workable structures which are likely to produce behaviour leading to the achievement of goals, and the ways in which control is successfully exercised, will demand other kinds of skills—management skills. A person who is a good teacher will not necessarily be a good manager, because he may not have the requisite knowledge and experience, nor the social skills to enable him to cope with the job of management. Of course, this is not to say that he cannot acquire them. At the present time, those school managers who do acquire those skills, acquire them in the course of doing a management job. If, instead, some effort were made to structure the learning process so that they were helped to acquire these skills before their appointment, or as soon as possible afterwards, it is reasonable to assume that schools would be better managed as a result. In addition, we could be more certain in this case that requisite skills would be acquired (in so far as we can determine what those skills are), rather than leaving the learning process to the good luck and judgement of those concerned.

In the third place, we might expect consequences for the selection of school managers. If headmasters are recognized as managers, those involved in the selection and appointment of headmasters might be in a better position to judge the suitability of candidates for management posts.

Some teachers might make a better contribution to schools by continuing to do what they can do best, that is, teaching. This is not to say that bad teachers should be appointed to management posts. Clearly, to be able to take the right kind of educational decisions for a whole school, a manager has to have a certain kind of experience, which would include taking educational decisions at a lower level. Perhaps one test of this is to be a good teacher. Furthermore, all teaching involves management skill in the sense of deciding on the allocation of the teacher's and the pupil's resources in ways likely to lead to the pupil's learning what the teacher wants him to learn. Or, to put it another way, the teacher has to structure the situation in such a way that it is most likely to lead to the achievement of the teaching goal. At the organizational level, however, the situation is correspondingly more complex and the manager needs different kinds of knowledge, experience, and skills. An assessment has to be made of whether the candidate has the knowledge, experience and skills required to deal with the complexity, or whether he has the capacity to acquire them.

[11] Drucker, Peter: *The Practice of Management*, London, Pan Books (1968), p. 20.
[12] Taylor, F. W.; *Scientific Management*. Evanston, Harper and Row (1947).
[13] Maslow, A. H.; *Motivation and Personality*, New York, Harper and Row (1954).
[14] McGregory D.; *The Human Side of Enterprise*, New York, McGraw-Hill (1960).
[15] Herzberg, F. Mausner, B., Snyderman, B. B.; *The Motivation to Work*, New York, Wiley (1959).
[16] Bradley, D. and Wilkie, R.; *The Concept of Organization*, Glasgow, Blackie (1974).

CHAPTER 6

Pastoral Guidance Systems: A Case Study

An attempt has been made to present an organizational analysis of the school, which, by necessity, has been of a general nature, although some illustrations have been given. The merit of such an analysis may be more clearly indicated by considering in some detail the introduction into Scottish schools of systems of pastoral guidance. Not only is this a relatively recent development, but it is also one that has important implications for schools over the next decade.

During the 1960s some Scottish schools experimented with systems of pastoral guidance. The aim was to achieve closer and more effective contact with pupils, in order to overcome some of the disadvantages of the larger school. Teachers were appointed as housemasters and housemistresses and pupils were allocated to houses. The house staff were to assume responsibility for the pastoral guide of the pupils. In 1971 the Scottish Education Department produced a paper[17] proposing the establishment of pastoral guidance systems for all secondary schools in Scotland. As a consequence of this and of a circular from the Department in 1972, most local education authorities in Scotland reorganized school staff structures and created pastoral guidance posts of some kind. The particular form of the system was left to the discretion of the local authorities. Teachers appointed to pastoral guidance posts were henceforward officially styled principal teachers (and assistant principal teachers). In other words, they were to have the same title as heads of departments. The older nomenclature however, still survives.

The effect of this measure has varied in different schools. Local authorities have instituted different systems, for example, and headmasters have shown varying degrees of support and encouragement for the new system and its staff. The amount of non-teaching time allocated to guidance staff for the performance of their guidance duties has varied as have the facilities put at their disposal. An obvious difference occurs between, on the one hand, schools recently built with a guidance system in mind, where, for example, house blocks may exist with dining facilities, offices for house staff, interview room and discussion rooms, and pupil areas clearly identified in the minds of pupils and teachers as belonging to a 'house'; and, on the other hand, schools which may already be short of space and which have to find additional space for the new guidance staff.

Guidance staff vary in the activities in which they become involved, in their methods of working and in the emphasis they put on different activities. Much depends, of course, on the particular system which is in operation. In a vertical system, where pupils of all ages are found in each house, all house staff will be involved with much the same sorts of activities. In a horizontal system, on the other hand, where guidance staff have responsibility for year groups, we might expect those responsible for the middle or senior schools to be concerned with different activities from those responsible for the junior pupils. Broadly speaking, however, guidance staff will be involved in the following activities. They make contact with new pupils, perhaps by visiting primary schools before the pupils arrive at the secondary school. They meet parents on formal occasions such as parents' evenings, when parents may be invited as well as on occasions when parents ask for personal interviews, or when parents of individual pupils are asked to come to the school for discussions. Some guidance staff also visit pupils' homes if they think it necessary. They are often involved in discipline problems although an effort may be made to isolate them from routine discipline problems. They may give broad careers and curricular advice. They record information on pupils and write internal reports and reports for employers. They may institute a system of regular meetings with individual pupils, and they are often involved with the personal problems of pupils. They may run extra-curricular activities, and they often have contacts with outside agencies such as social services departments.

As a result of all this, we can say that Scottish secondary schools now have a goal of providing pastoral guidance for their pupils. This official goal and the structure which went with it was imposed on the schools. No school had the choice of accepting or rejecting the goal. There was, of course, much discussion of the proposals when they were first published, but this did not amount to the possibility of choice by individual schools. An important publication in the debate which led to this situation was a pamphlet published in 1968 by the Scottish Education Department, entitled 'Guidance in Scottish Secondary Schools'[18]. The term guidance was used to denote

> "The taking of that personal interest in pupils as individuals which makes it possible to assist them in making choices or decisions. The choices which pupils will have to face involving situations of various kinds; deciding which school subjects to continue or to take up or to drop, selecting one type of career as a vocational aim in preference to another, weighing up the merits of different courses of action."

The pamphlet points out that many teachers have always taken a personal interest in their pupils, but

> "many claims are . . . made on a teacher's time and in the stress of other work even the most sympathetic teacher may fail to notice that a particular pupil would benefit from advice or help".

Following comprehensive reorganization there will be more large schools, and consequently "the problem of ensuring adequate personal attention to every pupil has become more acute . . .".

Other reasons are given why guidance "has become essential at the present time".

> "As has frequently been pointed out, young people are now subjected to stresses which did not affect their predecessors. They have to face the increasing complexity of modern life. Television, radio, films, books, newspapers have made them aware of matters of which they would formerly have known little or nothing. Many have a measure of financial independence which makes them a natural target for commercial propaganda, often before they are ready to deal objectively with it. The removal of certain fears and sanctions has made it easier for young people to assert themselves and challenge authority. The natural tendency of young people to rebel is aggravated by the gap between the generations, which has resulted largely from the rapidity of technological advance and social change. Finally, despite their apparent self-assurance, young people often experience a feeling of general insecurity and uncertainty and need help and support in their search for satisfying criteria on which to base the conduct of their daily life".

This is seen as a problem for society as a whole, "but it is right and inevitable that the schools should play a major part in helping to solve it". In doing this they should be prepared to co-operate with other agencies. "Above all they should enlist the help of parents". In cases where parents may not be able to cope with their children or where they may not be interested, "it is particularly important that the school should be able to offer young people the guidance they might otherwise lack and should do its utmost to compensate for any inadequacy in the advice and support given by the home".

Four distinct goals are clearly being advocated by the Department: pupil guidance, helping in the solution of a social problem, co-operation with other agencies, and compensation for parents whose advice and support for their children may be 'inadequate'. It is perhaps the last of these four goals which is the most striking. Who is to say which parents are inadequate? How is inadequacy to be defined? Most people would agree on certain criteria. If children are being neglected in terms of food and shelter and if this can be properly blamed on the parents, or if children are being physically ill-treated, then we could agree that their parents are in some sense inadequate. Although even here there would be a wide variety of opinion as to what constituted, for example, physical ill-treatment, or to the extent to which neglect could be attributed to the parents alone. Nevertheless, perhaps we can say that there are certain basic standards which have to be adhered to, or else the courts may interfere. It is significant, however, that it is only on very basic issues that we can say that such agreement exists. There is still a very large area of discretion left to individual parents as to the way they bring up their children. Obviously, the writers of the pamphlet have in mind issues other than such basic ones, if only because other agencies, such as social welfare agencies and the courts, are involved in cases of neglect or physical illtreatment. In which case there is still the problem of defining inadequacy.

There is, of course, no objective definition of inadequacy. A school's assessment of parental inadequacy, perhaps based on limited contact with children and their parents, will be subject to human error. What standards are parents being judged against? Are there dangers in working-class parents being judged by and according to the standards of middle-class teachers? Are these judgements likely to be adequate themselves? Important issues are also raised by the goal of helping in the solution of a social problem.

Why is it 'right and inevitable' for schools to do this? Are they equipped for such work? It may, of course, be inevitable that schools will become involved in such activity because they have to cope with children's behaviour which results from the problem and also because teachers are the only set of adults apart from parents themselves, who are in close and continuing contact with children.

The guidance systems, then, were established with goals which were less than clear-cut, and in these circumstances we might expect to find disagreement within the schools. Some teachers have reacted to these developments on the grounds that schools are being over-extended and that much of this activity should be the province of social work agencies. Others say that individual teachers did the sort of job that was necessary in cases of, for example, lateness or maltreatment, without the necessity for new structures which may detract energy from what should be the school's major task, that of teaching. These reactions reflect an uneasiness as to what schools should be doing, in other words about the goals of the schools. Teachers agree that pupils ought to acquire a certain body of knowledge by the time they leave school, although what that body of knowledge should be in practice will vary according to the perceived abilities of the pupils. Beyond that there is confusion and disagreement. Some teachers, for example, think that if the school is involved officially in personal guidance there is a danger of prying into the pupils' background and invading the privacy of pupils and their families. On the other hand teachers have long recognized that a pupil's home background will affect his performance in school. Therefore, the argument goes, schools are bound to be concerned with more than just the academic progress of their pupils because that very progress is affected by other factors.

There is also some disagreement as to what is involved in pupil guidance. Career or vocational guidance may be included, but the guidance staff may not be involved in this except in the broadest sense. There may, for example, be a careers master or some other person who looks after the careers literature which comes into schools and who gives detailed career advice. Pupils also need guidance as to the courses they are going to take within the school, but again schools vary in the degree to which guidance staff are involved in this. In practice the decision as to which course individual pupils follow will probably be taken by the headmaster or his deputy or an assistant headmaster or some group within the school, although the guidance staff may be consulted about individual pupils. Personal guidance is almost universally recognized as the province of the guidance staff but what is actually meant by this is the subject of much disagreement.

The uneasiness and disagreements over the aims of the new systems have sometimes contributed to difficult relationships between guidance staff and other teachers, particularly between the guidance staff and the heads of departments. Some heads of departments said that they did not know what the house staff did or what the new system was supposed to do. There was a feeling that the role of the school was being expanded to include something like social work. A typical comment was made by one principal teacher when he said that it was a question of whether the schools were to become social centres with education secondary or whether education should be primary with the rest secondary. He was in favour of the schools having an education function with guidance only as an accessory. Another principal teacher said that the schools ran well enough without the house staff. He thought the way things were going education would be up the spout. They ought to get back to the three Rs. Things were changing and so they ought to change their ideas, but there were too many frills. One principal teacher thought that most pupils were normal and neither required nor welcome intrusion into their affairs. There were a few who benefited, but he found it incredible to set up a tremendous structure for the few.

Disagreement may have centred on the aims of the system, but the workings of the system were also criticized. Some principal teachers saw house staff as excessively secretive. One principal teacher attributed what he saw as the unco-operativeness of the principal teachers to the secrecy and confidentiality of the house staff. Another, while agreeing that much of the work of the house staff was confidential, nevertheless thought that they did not receive enough information from them. One principal teacher, who thought that contact with the house staff could be helpful, added that he was not happy about feedback between house staff and principal teachers. The house staff in this school, although they thought it necessary to know a lot about a child's background, were reluctant to pass this information on to other teachers, although they would pass on as much as they thought appropriate. A housemaster said that they were prepared to release information to other teachers where they thought the information might be useful in the classroom situation, but they would not talk freely about a child's background simply in the course of conversation. He thought that teachers sometimes asked for information simply out of curiosity. This situation may have been exacerbated by the early difficulties encountered by the house staff. One housemistress said that when they were first appointed, people asked what they did and when they tried to explain, which was difficult because of the nature of the job, people would say, yes, but what do you really do? As a result of this they tended to stick together. Relations between the house staff in this school remained close.

There were also difficulties over communications. In one school where there was no joint meeting between house staff and subject principals, this was viewed unfavourably from both sides, although particularly by the house staff. The meeting they had with the headmaster was not, in their opinion, very useful. They were not allowed to take part in policy decisions and the meeting had a limited usefulness for information purposes. The head, however, thought that the business of the two meetings was quite different. The house staff treated the separate meetings as a reflection on their status. A housemaster said that such an arrangement separated them from the rest of the promoted staff, and the fact that their meeting was held during the lunch break put the status of the house staff and their meeting on a different level. This housemaster thought they should have a definite say in the decision-making processes of the school. Principal teachers, he thought, often had an axe to grind and had a narrow restricted view, whereas the house staff were more concerned with the whole school.

As a result of this, most contact between principal teachers and house staff was confined to informal meetings at lunch or in passing. By the nature of the job, house staff have to be in contact with a large number of staff for a variety of reasons. The special circumstances of the school, however, mean that meetings are often difficult to arrange. Other teachers may be teaching when the housemaster is free and so they tend to take the opportunity of talking to people they wish to see whenever that occurs. They may often be late for classes as a result. They may also be called away from classes to attend to parents who arrive unexpectedly, or children who are causing problems, and this means that their teaching is frequently interrupted. Some subject principals have tended to interpret this as a conflict of loyalties on the part of the house staff. Some have concluded that the house staff are not interested in teaching, and that they are concerned only about house business.

Status considerations were also involved, and an underlying factor in the situation concerned the fact that many of those appointed to guidance posts were holders of ordinary degrees, or else were teachers of subjects in which degrees were not awarded. In Scottish schools, principal teachers have traditionally enjoyed high prestige. This prestige has, in the main, been based on the fundamental requirements of an honours degree, on very long experience in teaching and, of course, on the fact that they were the heads of teaching departments. In recent years, this situation has been changing in that some teachers have been appointed to the headships of departments after just a few years of teaching in those subject areas where there is a shortage of teachers. The dramatic introduction of a new set of promoted posts in the form of housemasters and housemistresses has, however, been something else again. Not only was there now a new set of promoted posts of officially equal status to the heads of departments, but also the Scottish Education Department has proposed that for posts senior to principal teacher, in other words, assistant head, deputy head and head teacher, all holders of a Teaching Qualification in Secondary Education should be eligible. In this case, the new house staff were clearly eligible for promotion and were, therefore, in competition with heads of departments, who had until that time been the sole candidates.

One principal teacher said that, in his school, he thought the system was very useful because of the pupils at the school and the house staff who were among the best he had heard of. He used them quite a lot and trusted them. At this school there were no status problems as far as he was concerned. Although they might not have as high academic qualifications as he had, he did not see why they should not be paid as much; he admired their competence. In other schools, he might be aggrieved. There were some unfortunate appointments, he said, because for some it was their only line of promotion. He thought his attitude would depend on his impression of individual house staff.

The introduction of systems of pastoral guidance also indicates the importance of aspects of the environment, in this case the wider education system. The goals of the schools were altered. Pastoral guidance was no longer something which schools could choose to emphasize or to neglect. They now have an official goal of providing pastoral guidance for their pupils. The structural arrangements in schools were, of course, radically altered with the introduction of a new structure of pastoral guidance staff. Behaviour in schools was also affected. In the first place, those appointed to the new posts had a goal which was different from those of the rest of the staff. This is not to say that some schools and, in particular, some teachers had not previously made efforts in the area of pastoral guidance. The situation is clearly different, however, now that teachers have been appointed explicitly as guidance staff with extra non-teaching time allocated specifically for pastoral guidance duties.

Role expectations were also affected. A new set of role expectations had to emerge for the newly appointed staff. Some of the difficult relationships instanced above can be attributed in part to confusion and ignorance over role expectations. For the individuals appointed to these positions, there were a new set of expectations to be discovered. For those teachers who were not involved in guidance activities themselves, there were also new sets of expectations to be discovered. On the one hand, they had to discover what could be expected of the new staff. On the other hand, the role expectations attaching to their own positions were also altered by the appearance of new relationships. They were often expected to co-operate with the new staff by, for example, passing information to them about pupils. Principal teachers had to become used to having as members of their departments teachers with other major responsibilities. The situation was complicated by the fact that these members of their departments were theoretically, at least, of the same status as the principal teachers. In what ways would this affect the relationships between them? How would the situation affect the principal teachers' relationships with the other members of his department? If the new staff had major responsibilities outside their teaching duties, to what extent could they be expected or relied upon to make an appropriate contribution to departmental teaching? And what would be appropriate in these circumstances?

Heads of departments and guidance staff are, of course, concerned with different goals and activities in the school. Their own professional and day-to-day concerns may lead them to emphasize the importance of the goals and procedures of the school with which they are most intimately concerned. Heads of departments may emphasize the importance of academic teaching, and thereby the primacy of their own departments, whereas the house staff may stress the importance of getting to know each child and helping him to solve his problems. As both activities call on the resources of the school, in terms of time and staff, the possibilities for conflict are obvious.

The situation was open to amelioration or aggravation by other factors. Much depended, for example, on the particular individuals appointed to the new position and their reaction to the situation. Some who were clearly committed to the new ideas and who were recognized as competent teachers in their own right may have had less difficulty in establishing satisfactory relationships. Others were alleged to have taken the jobs simply because their qualifications made it unlikely that they would have been promoted to departmental headships, and were, therefore, less deserving of respect. Another factor in the situation concerned age and facilities of the school. In new schools where the staff were brought together for the first time, it may have been easier for them to accept new goals and to establish easy relationships with the guidance staff. Newly built schools were also more likely to have special facilities for the guidance staff. In older schools on the other hand, which had recognized ways of working and perhaps an established body of tradition, it may have been more difficult to assimilate new goals and new staff appointed specifically to work for the achievement of these goals.

A third factor in the situation was the managerial response. Some undoubtedly shared the feelings of unease which accompanied the introduction of the new systems, and had their doubts about the role which schools were being asked to play in the area of pupil welfare. On the other hand, their position in the schools may have made it easier for them to see any benefits which accrued from the new arrangements. Their own goal priorities were, of course, greatly affected by the imposition of a major new official goal. The structural arrangements which may have appeared to work well previously might also now prove inadequate. What new structural arrangements were necessary? Should there be regular meetings of the guidance staff under the chairmanship of the headmaster or some other person? Who was to have overall charge of the guidance system? When were meetings to be held? Could they be fitted into the timetabled activities of the school or should they take place outside school hours? What effect would the new system have on the established activities of the school? In what ways would teaching be affected? What changes would be advisable or necessary in the arrangements for extra-curricular activities? Certain procedures might be more affected than others—for example, over discipline and the collecting and recording of information about pupils.

As might be expected, headmasters' responses have varied. It was said earlier that the amount of non-teaching time allocated to guidance staff for the performance of their guidance duties has varied. So has the degree of freedom which headmasters have allowed guidance staff to develop the units in their charge in different ways. Some headmasters think it valuable for houses (if that is the adopted system) to develop in individual ways according to the desires and abilities of the staff in charge of each.

Others are concerned that if the houses become too differentiated, pupils will identify more with the house to which they belong than with the school. They may, therefore, exercise greater control over the house system in the interests of standardization and lay greater emphasis on the school's extra-curricular activities than on house activities.

Some headmasters have decided to develop a formal guidance programme, which may include a period set aside in the timetable where groups of pupils discuss topics which come under the heading of 'social education'. These topics may include a wide variety of aspects of living and working in modern society. In such a programme the entire staff of the school, and not just the guidance staff, may be involved. Other headmasters resist this attempt to 'raise guidance to the level of a subject'. They see difficulties in asking staff to involve themselves formally in something for which they have no training and in which they may have no particular interest. Other headmasters are adopting a wait and see policy. They may be broadly in favour of the idea but conscious of the difficulties in finding a formula which is useful and acceptable.

With regard to the conflict which emerged or which was latent in the situation, headmasters adopted varying strategies. One headmaster instituted a joint meeting of subject principals and house staff in an attempt to achieve the conciliation of conflicting requirements. Another headmaster held meetings of house staff, which he chaired, outside school hours in order to show the other staff that the house staff had no soft job. The reinforcement given to the guidance staff did not always work in the way it was intended. For instance, one headmaster sent a memo to all staff urging them to pass on to the house staff information about pupils regarding achievements, poor attendance, illness of parents, bad behaviour, accidents, poor health, and similar themes. He went on to say that the passing of this information would not necessarily be taken as a reference for action, but was meant to ensure that the house staff had up-to-date information on the children. Staff should use the special slips available for passing on such information. One principal teacher said later that he did not think that the official forms were much used. He could spend half his day doing this, telling the house staff about smelly feet, scratching and peculiarities of behaviour, but he did not. He did not make official contact with the house staff. Any contact with them was casual. Almost because of the headmaster's underlining of official contact he had stopped doing this, he said. He thought the house staff might be finding their jobs difficult as he did not know if they were getting information from the principal teachers. He, for one, could not be bothered filling in forms, it was easier to mention things in passing.

The control aspect of management is also affected by the new system. In one sense, control may be made easier, particularly in larger schools, where there are possibilites of closer and more regular contacts with individual pupils. Those who may be having difficulties with their work may be more easily spotted if a housemaster is able to put together information received from a number of subject teachers about the pupil's poor performance. It may also be easier to help with personal problems which might otherwise interfere with the pupil's work. However, there are also difficulties of control. For example, there are questions about the degree of difference which should be allowed to develop between houses. To what extent should the information collected by various houses be standardized? If the school has a horizontal system, what kind of co-ordination is needed between the guidance staff as pupils move up the school (unless guidance staff also move up the school with the pupil year groups)? There is also the question of how guidance activities are to be evaluated. Does the headmaster judge by the degree of knowledgeability the guidance staff have about their pupils, by the extent of house activities which are developed, or according to some estimate of the atmosphere of the house? Control is an important problem in most organizations. Efforts to solve the problem will require assessments of structural changes which may be necessary and a realization of the importance of selection and training of the members of the organization. Ultimately, however, these efforts will depend for their degree of success on an organizational perspective. It is hoped that this introductory book will have helped to indicate the usefulness of such a perspective.

[17] Scottish Education Department: *The Structure of Promoted Posts in Secondary Schools in Scotland,* Edinburgh, H.M.S.O. (1971).

[18] Scottish Education Department: *Guidance in Scottish Secondary Schools,* Edinburgh, H.M.S.O. (1968).

Suggestions for Further Reading

Those who wish to inquire further into organization theory may find the following texts useful:

Bradley, D. and Wilkie, R. *The Concept of Organization*, Glasgow, Blackie (1974)

March, J. G. (ed), *Handbook of Organizations*, New York, Rand McNally (1965)

Etzioni, A. (ed), *A Sociological Reader on Complex Organizations* (2nd edition), New York, Holt, Rinehart and Winston (1970)

Those interested in organization theory as applied to the school should consult the following:

Hughes, M. D. (ed), *Secondary School Administration: A Management Approach*, Oxford, Pergamon Press (1970)

Cicourel, A. V. & Kitsuse, J. I., *The Educational Decision-Makers*, New York, Bobbs-Merrill (1963)

Shipman, M. D., *The Sociology of the School*, London, Longmans, Green (1968)

Bidwell, C. E. 'The School as a Formal Organization', in J. G. March (ed): *Handbook of Organizations*, New York, Randy McNally (1965)

Banks, O., *The Sociology of Education*, London, Batsford (1971)